A Man & His Truck

How I Shared the Gospel in the Towing Industry

Robert U. Stuart

A Man & His Truck

To order books, send a check or money order
payable to Robert Stuart for $15.00 per book
with your name and address to:
A Man & His Truck
P.O. Box 105
Kernersville, NC 27285-0105

ISBN 978-0-615-36158-1

Library of Congress Control Number: 2010903657

All scripture references in this publication are from The King James Version of the Bible (KJV).

Cover photography by Stacey Holt.
Cover and book design by Anna Stuart Wright.
Photo restoration by Anna Stuart Wright and Eric Christopher Wright.
Inside photographs reproduced by Horizon Graphics, Inc.

First Edition
Set in New Baskerville

Printed in the United States of America by:
Faith Printing
4210 Locust Hill Road
Taylors, SC 29687

A Man *&* His Truck

How I Shared the Gospel in the Towing Industry

ROMANS : 5 : 8

Dedications

DEDICATIONS

To my father, Ned Russell Stuart, Sr.,

who taught me so much as I worked by

his side for many years.

To my wonderful wife, Rebecca,

who has been my partner for 52 years.

Her patience, love and understanding have kept me going.

To my son, Russ Patrick Stuart and

daughter, Anna Stuart Wright,

who inspired me to write this book.

To my grandchildren, Rally Robert,

Collin Russ and Carlee Colleen Stuart,

who I hope will enjoy my stories for years to come.

Contents

CONTENTS

Acknowledgements
ACKNOWLEDGEMENTS

First of all, I want to acknowledge my wonderful Lord and Savior, whose written word motivates me and fills my heart and mind with scriptures and thoughts I desire to share with others.

I am grateful to my daughter, Anna Stuart Wright, and son-in-law, Eric Christopher Wright, both graphic artists, who knew how to design and assemble this book. This endeavor would not have been possible without their expertise.

Faydene Williard Long, my sister-in-law, took a special interest in my book and offered her support. She spent many hours transcribing my rough draft.

Danny Fritts, a long-time friend and many times a co-worker, always challenged me to write about my life experiences. I may never have written this book without his encouragement.

My thanks to all the unsung heroes who helped bring my book to completion.

A Tribute

A TRIBUTE

In Remembrance of my Brother,

Lt. Colonel Ned Russell Stuart, Jr.

July 2, 1930 - September 1, 1992

*N*ed was a graduate of N.C. State University with a B.S. degree in Industrial and Mechanical Engineering. He began his civilian career as a Captain for Eastern Airlines and was, at the time of his death, the chief pilot and  manager of the Aviation Department for Burlington Industries. He was a board member of the National Business Aircraft Association, Missionary Aviation Institute and Piedmont Bible College. Ned's military service included work as a base test pilot/instructor at the Jet Fighter School at Williams AFB, Arizona; Senior Maintenance Officer of the Combat Operations Staff, (HQ USAF), Washington, D.C.; and Admissions Liaison Officer for the United States Air Force Academy. He was a recipient of the Meritorious Service Medal. He retired in 1983 after 30 years of military service. Ned's wife, June Johnson Stuart and their son, Bryan Weaver Stuart, now make their home in Tennessee.

Foreword
FOREWORD

BY RUSS STUART

My father, Robert Stuart, grew up in Kernersville, North Carolina, surrounded by automobiles, tow trucks and fire trucks. In the 1920s, his father, Ned R. Stuart, Sr., owned and operated Stuart Motor Company, an automobile repair shop. By 1930, the company had evolved into the city's first Ford dealership and soon added a towing and recovery service complete with a Model T tow truck.

Stuart Sr. also organized the town's first fire department and served as chief for many years. Their facility housed the town's first fire truck. Dad remembers as a very small boy earning a quarter a week for opening the big garage doors. He and his brother, Ned Jr., grew up working on cars and watching their father handle emergencies.

Dad's mother, Annabel Lemon Stuart, was from Roanoke, Virginia. She was head of nursing at Baptist Hospital in Winston-Salem, N.C. during the 1920s. She later worked for the Forsyth County Health Department and was involved with social services. Annabel was very active in the community, serving with the Red Cross and Civil Defense. Dad got his love of people from his mother, Annabel, who passed away in 1948 at the age of 44 when he was 14 years old.

The first tow truck Dad remembers is the big monster he operated until 2007, a 1943 Sterling with a long crane on the rear. He and his father repainted the crane red and black, built a platform on the back and added a huge Tulsa winch, 1,000 feet of cable, several log chains, snatch blocks, cable slings of varying lengths and blocks of wood for cribbing. This extraordinary vehicle, rich with history, was designed to move B-29s off runways for the U.S. Navy but was never used overseas. The Stuarts purchased the wrecker in 1947 from the U.S. Government's War Assets and Administration Department in Charleston, S.C., where it swapped engines on planes in the Charleston Navy yard. It still has the original engine and clutch. The engine has been overhauled only once. The wrecker has been in the Stuart family wrecker and recovery business for 63 years. Through the years, it set eight airplanes back on runways, winched out bulldozers embedded in deep mud and uprighted tractor-trailers on major interstates. Interesting contents that some of the tractors and trailers were loaded with included: TVs, tomatoes, aspirin tablets, soft drinks, screws, cabbage, liquid rubber, pizzas, pigs, cement, lumber, mirrors, aquariums, glass, mattresses, gas, furniture, morgan pipe, fishing supplies, liquid grease, rice, brick, bales of cotton, rolls of paper, batteries, crayons, milk, chickens, steel beams, meat, wood and furnishings for the Turkish embassy insured for $21 million dollars.

Dad served in the Korean War as a military policeman and spent the last nine months of duty in Alaska. He graduated from UNC Chapel Hill with a degree in education and then taught school and coached sports but later decided to join his father to help run the business. After his father's death, Dad ran his own towing and recovery business for 22 years. He is also a former fire chief and building inspector for the town of Kernersville. My dad, like my grandfather, wore many hats.

After much persuasion, our family talked Dad into retiring in November of 2007. He is enjoying retirement, and we are enjoying spending more time with him. My dad has been an encouragement to me, and his determination has taught me to never give up. He showed me, by example, that hard work is rewarding, and family is precious. Most importantly, I learned to trust the Lord regardless of the circumstances. I hope you will be inspired by his unusual approach to people, his work and how he shared the gospel.

-Russ Stuart

Introduction
INTRODUCTION

During my 59 years in the towing and recovery industry, I have had the wonderful opportunity to share the gospel with others. I have met many precious Christians from all over the country, and we encouraged each other from the scriptures. I met others who admitted they did not know the Lord. They were just trying to do the best they could and trusting in their church membership as I once did. Witnessing lives turned around was the greatest joy in my experiences.

Along the way, I have found humor in dangerous situations. The Lord has been with me all this time and kept me safe. This book is a collection of stories that tell some of my experiences over the years. I hope it will encourage wrecker men as well as people from all walks of life.

All cities and towns mentioned in the book are located in North Carolina unless otherwise stated.

Chapter 1. **And A Little Child Shall Lead Them**

It was a Sunday afternoon, the Lord's day. My son, Russ, and I were busy trying to upright a toy tractor and trailer that had turned over on the living room rug. Russ was about six years old. I had already started teaching him how to rig chains and cables. I would strap him in a car seat and take him with me in the wrecker at various times when I wasn't very busy and had a short trip.

One of the things I taught Russ early on was always to play it safe, to look ahead at what might happen and try to prepare for it. One of the things I taught him was to scotch wheels so they would not roll. Now, you have heard the saying: "Practice what you preach!"

We started winching the tractor and trailer. Russ immediately stopped me and said "DAD! We have to scotch the wheels so the rig won't slide!" I told him, "Son, in a real situation you won't have to scotch them because the rubber tires usually dig in the dirt or pavement and will scotch themselves." Nevertheless, Russ insisted that we scotch the wheels, so I played along.

The next day, at 6:00 a.m., I got a call about a tractor and trailer that had overturned with its load of lumber on a bridge in Kernersville. We all know when it is very cold, as it was that morning, the surface of a bridge freezes first when it starts to snow. That was the situation when I arrived. The rig was turned over in the westbound lane, right in the middle of the bridge.

I could not position the wrecker perpendicular to the rig as it should be; therefore, I started rigging to the concrete bridge railings. I doubled back five times with my cables and anchored to three of the railings. As I started lifting up the rig, everything was going smoothly, or so I thought. I had it up within about two feet from touchdown, where it would fall over. All of a sudden, the tires slipped on the icy surface, and the trailer fell back down. I remembered that my son told me to scotch the wheels. After much energy and stress re-rigging the tractor and trailer, I scotched the wheels by chaining them to a guardrail. After breaking two five-eighths inch chains, I finally turned up the rig.

How did I break two chains? At that time, I had not invented the corset trick which you will learn about later. I'm glad I finally remembered the advice of my son, "Scotch the wheels, Dad!"

Isaiah 11:6 "...and a little child shall lead them."

Chapter 2. **Death Row**

This is a story about a man I have never forgotten because of his testimony of how the Lord saved him in a wonderful way. One morning a truck driver came to Roadway Express with a load of jiff locks. The foreman called me to unload them. When I arrived, I met the truck driver and immediately realized there was something remarkable about this man.

I always try to get a conversation started to see if a person is a Christian. The Lord had a wonderful blessing in store for me. The truck driver began to tell me about his life. When he returned from serving his country in World War II, he had gotten caught up in the bootlegging business selling white liquor. He said that was the only way he had to earn money. After a time, a deputy sheriff started provoking him and picked on him unmercifully. The truck driver considered it to be a sort of persecution. One day he had enough and fatally shot the deputy. He told me that shooting the deputy didn't bother him anymore than if he had killed a dog. I was shocked! He ended up on death row.

The truck driver told me that one day another prisoner on death row was led out of his cell to be executed. The truck driver walked by the prisoner's empty cell and noticed a Bible lying on a table. The trucker pretended to go into the other inmate's cell by "mistake" so he could get the Bible. He began reading in Genesis. When he got to the story about Joseph, he was convicted of his sins.

The truck driver repented and asked the Lord into his heart and was saved. When he got to the book of Romans, he had full assurance of his salvation. This man did not have a lot of education, but he knew he needed the Lord.

I was amazed at the grace of God and how He had saved this sinner. I was so thrilled at his testimony that I gave him a hug and told him that I would be back in about 30 minutes. I went home and got a special Bible and some commentaries for him because he said he had become a minister of the gospel.

My friend also told me there was never a day that went by that he did not pray for the family of the deputy that he had killed. He also said that according to the scriptures, he knew the Savior had forgiven him, and his home would be in heaven. This man did not have much, but he had spiritual wealth because he had the Lord as his Savior. The truck driver was saved in a marvelous way, and he had become a child of the King. Before parting, we agreed to pray for each other. I never knew how he got out of prison.

Psalm 118:23 "This is the Lord's doing; it is marvelous in our eyes."

Chapter 3. **Get Back**

It was one of those sweltering, hot August days. A call came in concerning a tractor and trailer that was down an embankment near a creek off of Westchester Drive in High Point. Upon arriving, my dad and I saw that the tractor had separated from the trailer at the fifth wheel. Before we began winching, we told the bystanders to get back for their safety.

We winched the tractor out immediately. Then we backed up to the edge of the embankment and doubled back with our cables three times to the trailer. The trailer was loaded with 55 gallon barrels of old batteries that were heavy as lead.

We started winching the trailer. Dad and I had some special signals that we used to communicate with each other. Using one of his signals, Dad told me to put the winch in a lower gear because it was pulling extremely hard. We had run an anchor line to a tree across the road in the woods. I would always put one foot on the brake and one on the accelerator. Again we cautioned the bystanders to get back as some of them had not heeded our first warning. I had the wrecker in second gear, and the cables were pulling hard. As I looked out the back window, the anchor cable broke, and it seemed that the big wrecker jumped clear off the ground! I looked around just in time to see the end of the cable headed toward the woods. Needless to say, we did not have to remind anyone to "get back" anymore!

Ezekiel 33:5 "He heard the sound of the trumpet, and took not warning; his blood shall be upon him. But he that taketh warning shall deliver his soul."

Chapter 4. **The Patient**

One afternoon, I went to visit my friend, Charlie Barnard. Charlie had worked for me, and I still consider him one of the best mechanics I have ever known. He also had a tremendous amount of common sense. It was a privilege to work with Charlie. As Charlie and I were talking, he reminded me of an incident in High Point that occurred when we were recovering a tractor and trailer. One lane of Highway 29-70 was closed down. We were waiting for the company to decide whether or not to unload a trailer full of paper.

Walt Idol, who helped me for many years, was with us that day. Walt showed up wearing a white service manager's uniform. He decided to lie down in the shadow of the back of the big wrecker and take a nap while we were waiting for the company to make a decision. Now, try to picture the situation. A large crowd was standing around observing. There was the big rig turned over on its side, the High Point Police Department, the highway patrol, Charlie, me, and there was Walt taking a nap!

All of a sudden, a woman came up with an agitated look on her face. She had been observing all of us with the usual sidewalk supervision, or I should say, "superinten-dency." In her mind, all of us were standing around talking while Walt was lying down, unattended. She said, "Why don't you people get that man up from there and take him to the hospital?" She thought Walt was the one injured in the wreck because she mistakenly thought his white uniform was a sheet covering him. We could under-stand why she was concerned and irritated with us standing around!

I Thessalonians 5:6 "Therefore let us not sleep, as do others; but let us watch and be sober."

Chapter 5. **The Running Board**

I hesitated several times about whether to write this story, but I finally decided that it needed to be told. It is appropriate to tell about the predicaments wrecker men get into, even when it involves such a personal matter.

This incident occurred during the time I had to stay overnight for a week to care for my dad. He was a stroke victim paralyzed on his right side. About the middle of the week, White Motor Company wanted me to go to Chapel Hill to bring a garbage truck, which had caught on fire, back to their shop. My sister-in-law knew that I needed some help and volunteered her husband, Charles "Pink" Atkins, to go with me.

I took the Sterling, which ran about 40 mph and had no tow bar. It took most of the day. It was cold, and snow was on the ground. As we started back to Kernersville, I had to lower the boom about two feet to get under every bridge. When we reached Greensboro, Pink told me that he needed to relieve himself. I didn't want to stop because it was hard to get back up to the wrecker's top speed, especially on a major highway like I-40. I told him to try to wait just a little longer, and we would soon be in Kernersville. I didn't hear any more out of him until we were almost in front of White Motor Company. We only had about two more miles to go when he groaned, "I have to go now!"

White Motor Company faced I-40. To get to it, we had to go to the next exit and circle around a couple of blocks to reach the shop. Old trucks like mine had a big running board on which to stand. I told him to open the door and stand on the running board to relieve himself. It was cold, and I didn't think anyone would see him. Would you be brave enough to do what he did? I wonder if any wrecker man in the country has experienced the running board story. It took a lot of courage for Pink to do what he did.

Joshua 1:9 "Have not I commanded thee? Be strong and of a good courage; be not afraid, neither be thou dismayed: for the Lord thy God is with thee whithersoever thou goest."

Chapter 6. **The Terrible Stump**

A friend of mine called to ask if I would bring my small wrecker to his house and pull out a gum tree stump in his backyard. I wouldn't even try to pull a stump out with my small wrecker because it would not have enough power. Reuben told me that he had removed all the roots around the stump, and it would be easy to pull out. Reuben was a school teacher who knew nothing about stumps, and I was about to find out that I also knew nothing about stumps.

I told Reuben that it wouldn't cost any more to bring the big wrecker, so I took my Sterling. I positioned the wrecker in the backyard, backed up and doubled back one time with a snatch block. The stump was about five feet tall, and I thought it would come out fairly easy. I put my brakes on and set out my rubber scotches instead of the heavy ones because I didn't think I would need them. My first pull dragged my 41,000 pound wrecker up and over the rubber scotches. I backed off the scotches and put one set of the heavy scotches out and doubled back one more time. This pull also failed and pulled the wrecker over the heavy scotches. I couldn't believe it! I pulled up again, put out all four of the heavy scotches and doubled back one more time to a tree which I used for an anchor. This rigging now involved a six-part line. This time it came out with a tremendous amount of dirt. I lifted the heavy stump up and estimated it would weigh about eight tons. I carried it a short distance and left it on the side of the road.

When someone tells a wrecker man that a job will be easy, it will usually be just the opposite.

This was my first experience with a gum tree and I learned a valuable lesson. When you need a reliable anchor, find a gum tree; better still, let the Lord be your anchor!

Job 9:19 "If I speak of strength, lo, he is strong..."

Chapter 7. **We Did It!**

I had a call from Roadway to tow a tractor to Covington Diesel in Greensboro. Russ wanted to go with me, and since this was a short trip, I agreed to let him go. I had no reservations about Russ going with me because the big Autocar had a strong conventional front end which offered a lot of protection in case of an accident. This trip would also give us an opportunity to be together, and I could teach him a trade. I not only taught him how to hook up with chains, wear a yellow hard hat and scotch wheels with rubber scotches, but I would also talk to him about the Lord and the scriptures.

After we had finished a job in Greensboro, we were on our way back to Kernersville, and the traffic ahead was slowing down. I soon found out what the problem was: a loaded car carrier had gone off the road and was stuck in the median. A policeman flagged me down and asked me to winch it out.

There were two problems with this situation: I was in the Autocar, but I needed the Sterling to pull out the car carrier, and Russ was with me. I knew it would be a hard job, and I didn't know how he would react. Would he start crying? Would he get out of the Autocar while I was busy? I told the policeman I would give it the "old college try." I pulled the Autocar up to a steep embankment where I set up to winch the car carrier out. I had to position it as close to the embankment as possible, so I would have enough room to finish the job. It appeared to be about 20 feet deep. I was worried about Russ playing with the gears of the wrecker. I told him to sit still and not to touch anything while I was out of the truck. I put my heavy scotches out and started winching. As always, I asked the Lord to be my helper as my little helper had to sit still! The carrier came out with the first try.

I gathered all my equipment and got into the wrecker to leave. Russ looked at me and said, "We did it DAD! I love you DAD!" What a thrill! He was my great little helper although he only did one thing. He did just what was asked of him. This is exactly what the Lord wants us to do. He wants us to be faithful in all things. I Samuel 2:30 says, "...for them that honour me I will honour."

Colossians 3:20 "Children, obey your parents in all things: for this is well pleasing unto the Lord."

Chapter 8. What Is That Noise?

I received a call to go to Walnut Cove to pull a well driller out of the mud. I called Walt Idol, my old sidekick, and off we went. When we arrived, as always, a surprise awaited us. The well driller was stuck, but it was down a hill, and the service truck was also stuck beside it. We winched the driller out, but not without a lot of difficulty. Since it weighed about 60,000 pounds, I used three snatch blocks in my rigging. As it started up the hill, I heard an unfamiliar noise. Also, the cable seemed to have a strange vibration. We started to winch out the service truck. I had put the winch in a higher gear because it wasn't pulling as hard. All of a sudden I heard the noise again, but this time it was louder. I called down the hill to Walt and asked, "What is that noise?" He answered, "I don't know." Later, after we had winched the truck out and I was gathering my equipment, I accidentally found out what the noise was. When I uncoupled a snatch block, I saw the problem. The sheave was worn completely out and not running properly. It was grinding against the side of the block and making the noise.

When I arrived back home, I was still trying to figure out the reason why the sheave had gotten in such poor condition. All the snatch blocks had grease cups, and I always kept them greased fairly well. At the time, I carried 13 snatch blocks, and I inspected them all. I was surprised to find out that most of them were in bad shape. However, after some 30 years, I should not have been too shocked to find them in this condition.

After repairing the snatch blocks, it occurred to me what had caused the trouble. Years before, an Eastern Airlines plane skidded about 100 yards off the runway at the Greensboro Airport. The head of maintenance had called for several dump truck loads of crushed rock to be put in the muddy field behind the plane where Walt and I were going to winch it back on the runway. At the time, I thought they had put the wrong kind of rock down. It reminded me of a big water bed when the plane was pulled over it. The rock was full of grit. As a result of winching through the night and the following day, the grit acted like emery cloth and reamed out the bushings.

A wrecker man should always keep his equipment clean, which is very difficult to do at times. He also has to look out for everything—not only things to the right or to the left, but in front and behind. Most of all, he needs to be alert and listen carefully to every noise. We should always listen to the Lord and obey him.

Matthew 11:15 "He that hath ears to hear, let him hear."

Chapter 9. **You People**

The call came in about 7:00 a.m. from a trucking company in Greensboro. There was a tractor and trailer turned over on Highway 21 in Harmony. I called Walt Idol to go along with me. We drove to Statesville on Highway 158, then on to Harmony. This was before Interstate 40 was built. As a result, you can easily imagine how long it took us on an old two lane road with the Sterling traveling at 40 mph. I never went over 40 mph because it could have damaged the engine. We finally arrived at the wreck scene. Sure enough, the tractor and trailer was loaded with about 38,000 pounds of cotton bales and turned over in a ditch. After looking over the scene, I was glad that the Lord had conveniently placed some large white oak trees to anchor to exactly where I needed them.

This was one of my favorite jobs because it was such a great challenge. There was a lot of pressure on me, not only to turn the loaded rig back up, but to stand firm in what I knew was the right way to get the job done, in spite of considerable difficulties. A young patrolman came up and asked me what the plan was. I told him that since unloading the trailer with a fork lift was impractical, I would need to turn it up loaded. I also told him that I would have to block the road. He then asked me the question I often heard, "How long will it take?" I told him that since I had to turn it up loaded, it would take more time to rig, so no further damage would occur. He then inquired, "What if the side splits open?" I replied that I didn't think it would because of the compact load, but if it did, I would let it back down. After much explanation, he said, "Go ahead!" The thought came to me that a surgeon did not have to put up with "sidewalk superintendents" when he began an operation! I chose two sturdy oak trees and doubled back five times with my cables. I positioned the wrecker at an angle so that when the rig came up, I would be in the correct position to winch it out.

Everything went as planned, and the rig came up in excellent shape. It set down in a precarious way and still had a tendency to go back over. It was just at this juncture that the patrolman came up and made a startling statement, "You will have to let it back down—we have traffic backed up all the way to Elkin." I was stunned at his intervention. I quickly came to my senses and explained to him that I had saved a day of work, and the tractor and trailer was about ready to be pulled out onto the highway. He refused to listen and told me in no uncertain terms that I would have to let it back down!

He reminded me that I had said that I would let the trailer back down if the side started to split. I replied, "I said I would let it back down if it started to split, but it hasn't, and it would be ridiculous to set it down now because it could damage the rig." He told me if I did not let it back down he would take me to jail! I did not appreciate his threat, and it upset me. I did a good job, and there was no way that I was going to set the rig back down. I knew I had him where I wanted him. I was the only one that knew how to operate the old Sterling. Besides, if he took me to jail, who would finish the job?

About that time, a sergeant came up and told me that I would have to let it back down, or he would take me to jail! Walt came up and said something that surprised me. Before I tell you what Walt said, you need to know that I felt I didn't need any help from Walt, and I was holding my own. He was like my old dad; you would not want to mess with him. Walt was an older man who wore a deputy's badge and sometimes carried a gun. What did Walt say? He chewed the sergeant and the patrolman out! I didn't think I needed this aggravation, but in a way, it was funny. I was ready to go to jail because I sure wasn't going to let the trailer down!

What saved the day? At this juncture, the head man of the trucking company told the patrolman, "If Robert lets it down, it's yours in no uncertain terms." He had enough sense to put the responsibility on the patrolman if anything unfortunate happened. So the patrolman said, "Go ahead!" Walt and I continued our work. We checked the oil and cranked up the engine as I kept the cables tight, and we drove the rig out.

The sergeant came up to Walt and me and said, "Don't you people ever come up here again." I replied, "Don't worry. Since you showed us no courtesy, I would never come back." They just didn't get it. I thought we did an excellent job, and there was no damage to the trailer. They just didn't understand a wrecker man! I know patrolmen have their job and wrecker men have theirs. I can imagine the pressure on them when waiting on some wrecker operator to clear the highway. If we could all just work together, it would be so much easier.

Galations 5:15 "But if ye bite and devour one another, take heed that ye be not consumed one of another."

Chapter 10. **Saved By the Rock**

My brother-in-law, Lawrence Pope, called and told me that one of his tractor and trailer rigs was involved in an accident in Fancy Gap, Virginia. He informed me that the rig was loaded with Morgan pipe, and because of a brake failure, it had gone off the side of the mountain. At the time he called me, I was involved in moving machinery from the old Kernersville News building into their new building. At this point, I got an emergency call which was a house fire with a near fatality. Since I was with the fire department during this time, I needed to go. I left in a hurry and four hours later, I returned to finish the Kernersville News job. When I told my wife, Becky, I had to go to Fancy Gap the next morning, she was not too happy as I had already worked 36 hours straight due to back to back calls. However, she did understand that I needed to go help Lawrence. I told Lawrence that it would be the next day before I could go to Virginia. He told me that he would wait because the tractor and trailer was not going anywhere. I was glad because I had heard that Fancy Gap was a steep mountain, and I had never worked a wreck there before. I welcomed the challenge, although I never liked to take the Sterling wrecker that far which was about 65 miles at 40 mph.

Charlie Barnard (who worked for me at that time) and I started out early the next morning. Lawrence was to meet us there. When we were about halfway up the mountain, we saw the trailer off to the side of the road with the tractor hanging on a rock. After looking the situation over, I decided the best way to recover the rig was to block part of the road and winch it back off the rock with a lot of power. Three things were greatly in my favor: the rig was a single axle H model Mack, I had some grease with me, and I had a courteous and courageous Virginia State Trooper to block the road.

Remember, big trucks coming down the mountain would not be able to stop easily. I doubled back four times and put down my big scotches. I greased the rock and winched it back onto the road. When we looked around the tractor, we could not see the bottom of the mountain. The driver was fortunate to get out alive. He went to the hospital with minor injuries and was later released. I never knew how he opened the door and got out without falling down the mountain.

Needless to say, the rock saved this driver's life. When he had the accident, he probably didn't know his dangerous circumstances. I don't know whether he was a

Christian or not, but if he was, I am sure he would have appreciated the verse below.

Psalm 27:5 "For in the time of trouble he shall hide me in his pavilion: in the secret of his tabernacle shall he hide me; he shall set me up upon a rock."

Chapter 11. **Abraham Lincoln**

This story came about because a highway patrolman was getting aggravated with me when I was having a hard time on a tough job. In the old days, I always used the Sterling on a big wreck. For years, I made out without asking for any help. To do this, I had to learn the advantage of snatch blocks. Since I only had one large winch, my rigging had to be perfect. Once in a while, I would consider how great it would be if I had two winches to operate at the same time. I would have had the time of my life rigging cables everywhere!

I had doubled back four times on this job and decided I needed to double back one more time to do the job properly. It was just at this juncture that a hefty patrolman came up and asked, "Stuart, why do you keep changing your mind?" I answered him quickly, "Funny you asked me this question. I read in the newspaper last week that someone had asked Abraham Lincoln this same question." The trooper retorted, "What did he say?" I replied,

"Lincoln said that he was always thinking." The trooper got out of my sight and left me alone. It is always good to have an answer for sidewalk superintendents.

I Peter 3:15 "But sanctify the Lord God in your hearts: and be ready always to give an answer to every man that asketh you a reason of the hope that is in you with meekness and fear."

Chapter 12. **The Twins**

While on vacation one summer, I walked up the beach one morning to buy a newspaper and observed a father trying to push his twin sons in a heavy baby carriage through sand that was loose and soft. He was having a very difficult time as these were rather large boys. I was about to give him a hand since his wife was not helping him. However, I realized that we were headed in the same direction, and I decided to let him go in front of me. It occurred to me that this situation was an excellent analogy of how a wrecker operator should recover a vehicle from the sand. The first thing I did when I arrived on the scene of a wreck was to ask the driver how much weight was in the trailer. I didn't dare ask this dad how much the boys weighed, but I asked him how they were doing. He replied, "Oh, we're doing fine."

This dad was making it hard on himself. The front wheels sank out of sight and the carriage came to a halt.

First, he was lacking common sense. Second, he lacked experience operating "heavy" equipment. As a good sidewalk superintendent, I immediately had the solution to the problem. As all wrecker men know, he should have gone around to the front end of the carriage and pulled it up, raising the wheels as he did so. Push or pull? That was the question.

As I walked back up the beach, it occurred to me that when I was a teenager, my dad sent me on a wrecker call early one Sunday morning to pull a guy out of a mud hole which was located at the bottom of a hill. When I arrived, I witnessed two drunks attempting to resolve the situation. One was stuck at the bottom of the hill, and his buddy was at the top of the hill racing his engine. I didn't realize what was happening until the man in the old car at the top of the hill started to head down at a fast rate of speed. He was trying to push his buddy out of the mud. I couldn't believe what I was seeing. CRASH! BANG! This was the only time in over 59 years being in the wrecker business that pushing was more effective than pulling. At least he was moving it a little at a time. I wouldn't recommend this approach. It is better to pull a vehicle out instead of pushing it out unless you show up drunk in your wrecker. It might be a good experience for you, or it could be expensive.

I chose in this case of the two drunks not to say anything. I got in my wrecker and left these two alone in their folly. I have said many times that I never left a job, but this was one exception, and it spoiled my perfect record. There are two verses in Proverbs that appear to be a contradiction, but they really are not. The first says *not* to answer a fool in such an angry or rude way, thereby becoming a fool yourself. The second verse says that you *should* answer a fool to correct him of his lack of understanding.

Proverbs 26:4 *"Answer not a fool according to his folly, lest thou also be like unto him."*
Proverbs 26:5 *"Answer a fool according to his folly, lest he be wise in his own conceit."*

Chapter 13. **The Professional**

This incident occurred during a busy time at Roadway Express. New trucks were coming in to be undecked (unstacked). Sometimes, there were four four-ways to be undecked at one time. A four-way is a truck pulling three trucks stacked on top of each other. Used trucks were to be decked to go out to different places. After I undecked a four-way, the driver would go to the back lot, pull the axles and remove the exhaust pipe to be ready for me to deck him to go back out. To keep everything safe at this fast pace, I had to stay on my toes and make sure the driver did exactly what I told him. There had to be one boss, because if there were two opinions, there might be trouble. Once in a while, I ran into a person who thought they knew more than I did about running my business. I learned a lot about the wrecker industry in my 59 years of experience. Although a person can often learn something new from someone on the job, he has to go with what he knows is right.

After I had decked this driver, I asked him if the fifth wheel was locked properly. He informed me that he was a professional, and he knew what he was doing, but the Lord had a surprise waiting for him. After I had finished decking the trucks for him, I went inside to get a drink and was chatting with the shop manager while I was waiting on the next driver to get ready. Here came the "professional" and informed the foreman that there was a problem and that he wanted him to come out and look at the situation. He said there was some damage involved. I was concerned because I always double checked everything, so I wouldn't cause anyone to get hurt or cause any damage. I could not imagine what was wrong. I was beginning to think that somehow I was involved since I had just decked his trucks. When we got out to the lot, I knew immediately what went wrong. The "professional" did not have the saddle hooked on the fifth wheel properly, and when he drove off, the back truck fell down and damaged the oil pan causing the oil to leak out. A good policy is never to call yourself a professional until after retirement. I did not say a word, but the scripture verse below came to mind.

I Corinthians 10:12 "Wherefore let him that thinketh he standeth take heed lest he fall."

Chapter 14. **The Corset Trick**

A call came in one cold winter morning that a tanker loaded with liquid grease had overturned. Most of the load had leaked out of the manhole covers and covered the highway. It congealed because of the cold and was very slick. The tanker had completely blocked the road. I started my rigging to turn the entire rig back on its wheels. As I started to pull hard, the back pair of axles started to slide. I stopped and asked the firemen if they knew of anything that would dissolve the grease. One fireman told me to try hot water and then he went to get some. Sure enough, this melted the grease back into liquid.

I started to pull again. Everything was going well except for the back wheels on the tanker, which started to slide again. (I remembered I had the same problem on an icy bridge years before. I learned that day, after I had broken two five-eighths inch chains, that I needed a better procedure. I also remembered that I didn't hook low enough. For example, when I played football, if I got in a lower stance, I could handle the big guy in front of me. I learned about the law of leverage from reading a book on Judo.) Since those days, I had procured a short, wide nylon band about six feet long which reminded me of a wide corset used by women in the old days. I am no expert on corsets, but I know that a corset is worn by women around the middle of the body. If the corset were placed around the middle of the wheel, it would break when I started up with the rig. It is mandatory that it be located as low as possible for it to go around the bottom dual wheel that is on the ground. I put it around the outside tire next to the pavement and secured it back to the guardrail. This worked perfectly! The big rig came back over on its wheels. The "corset" worked like a charm, and that is why I carry one with me all the time. Be sure and *know* where to place a corset!

When I was chief of the fire department, I soon found out that I had to know and be sure about what I was doing or the result could be disastrous or deadly. I found this to also be true in the wrecker business.

I John 5:13 "These things have I written unto you that believe on the name of the Son of God; that ye may know that ye have eternal life, and that ye may believe on the name of the Son of God."

Chapter 15. Settled Out Of Court

White Motor Company called and wanted me to go to Ellerbe to recover a tractor and trailer which had overturned down an embankment. Up to that time, the longest trip I had made with the '43 Sterling was to Charlotte to winch an Eastern Airlines airplane back on the runway. At 40 mph, I didn't particularly want to go to Ellerbe, which was about 85 miles away. However, I considered this a real challenge, so I called my friend, Jay Lemmons, to go with me, and we left immediately.

When we arrived on the scene, the company was in the process of unloading the trailer which was loaded with all kinds of drinks. Everyone in the neighborhood was helping unload drinks from the trailer and loading them onto their pickup trucks. The manager of the tractor and trailer company decided to give each helper a few cases of drinks for their labor. The tractor and trailer had turned over down an embankment in a straight position, which meant that it would be easier to upright. There were some large pine trees across from the rig. I always like to think the Lord placed them there just for me. I asked the owner of the property in a nice way if I could anchor to his trees, and he agreed. I placed the Sterling at an angle so that when the trailer came up, I would be able to winch it up and out on the road all in the same rigging. Everything went just as I planned. It came up beautifully, and I pulled it up the road a short distance and started to hook it up to tow it home. About that time, the man who was so nice came up to me and said that my cables had damaged his fence. His fence was just an old rail fence, and I remember the cables moved some rails, but it involved no damage. The problem was not damage, but jealousy, because as he observed the scene, he saw others getting free drinks, and he wanted to get in on the action. I realized what he was up to, so I told him to talk to the manager and he would compensate him for the "damage." I believe he settled out of court for about six cases of drinks. How many people have settled out of court for such a small amount?

Jay and I put the rails back, and everyone was happy. After eating lunch, we towed the rig all the way back to Kernersville with no tow bar at 40 mph. In those days, we could get away without using a tow bar. In case you are wondering about the traffic backing up behind me on a two lane road, I pulled over now and then and let the traffic pass. When our family went to the beach every year, we drove by the exact location where the accident occurred. I would tell my kids about this story and they would say, "We know, Dad, you tell us every year!"

Deuteronomy 15:8 "But thou shalt open thine hand wide unto him, and shalt surely lend him sufficient for his need, in that which he wanteth."

Chapter 16. **Slow As Hell**

This story is about some experiences I had with a highway patrolman. One night, I received a call from the local police department that a car carrier had jackknifed off the road and that they needed a big wrecker. I called a friend to help me, and we started out, not realizing that the weather was bad and getting worse. The road was slick as glass, and to make matters worse, the police department gave me the wrong directions. It took me a while to find the location of the car carrier. When we arrived on the scene, the patrolman informed me that he had called another wrecker service. I told him that the dispatcher had given me the wrong directions, but this didn't change his mind. It was upsetting to be told to leave the scene since we came out on such a dangerous night, and the patrolman's attitude didn't help matters.

The second incident occurred one day about lunch time. The call came in that a tractor and trailer was stuck on a railroad track in Walkertown—a hurry-up call! I told the caller to inform the railroad to stop the train, and I would get there as soon as I could. I arrived on the scene without anyone to help me and put my heavy oak boards up under the wheels to build them up. I prepared to winch the rig out backwards because the left side of the trailer had fallen down into a deep hole. The same patrolman from the first incident came up suddenly and wanted to know if I needed any help. The rescue squad had called me and not the highway patrol. I told him that he needed to go down the road and keep the traffic away from me because there was a bad curve approaching the scene. Suddenly, another wrecker service arrived. This was the same company that the patrolman had called on that slick night years before. While I was working, I noticed the patrolman was talking with the truck driver. I was curious and asked the truck driver what the patrolman said about me. He relayed that the patrolman said I was good on small stuff, but not on big stuff. Of course the patrolman knew nothing about me, but I was learning a lot about him. If he only knew that I had pulled eight Eastern Airline planes back on the runway, he wouldn't have made that comment. You don't get any bigger "stuff" than that! After I winched the trailer out, the other wrecker company and the patrolman soon left.

The third incident involved a tractor and trailer that had turned over one morning a few years later. The highway patrol called me, and when I arrived, the same patrolman was there. The rig was loaded, but the trailer was a special trailer with holes to hook in at the top of it which made the job much easier. I doubled back twice and set it back on its wheels. A fireman came up about the time I finished getting all my equipment gathered and told me his dad knew me in the old days working a wreck on Highway 68 in High Point, near the Deep River Fire Department. I asked him the same question, "What did the patrolman say about me?" He replied, "You are the best, but are slow as hell!" The Holy Scriptures describe hell as a horrible place where there will be weeping and wailing. Will you go there, or will you trust the Lord as your Savior and have your sins forgiven and enter into the joy of the Lord forever?

Revelation 20:15 "And whosoever was not found written in the book of life was cast into the lake of fire."

Chapter 17. **Fools Rush In**

It was a cold, rainy and foggy Monday morning. I was enjoying my hot cup of coffee and oatmeal. The phone rang, and a teenager described to me how he had ended up in the creek beside the bridge at the Kernersville Lake on Old Valley School Road. I finished my breakfast, got in the Sterling and started to the scene. As I approached the bridge, I immediately saw the reason the boy wrecked. Approaching the bridge, I observed a fairly steep hill with a covering of trees providing shade, and the result was a frozen glaze on the road. I suspected this was what had caused the accident, so I took it extremely slow when I approached the scene. As I started down the hill, I put the wrecker in front-wheel drive. To my surprise, there was a jeep in the creek as well as the boy's car. I couldn't figure out why the jeep was there, but then I remembered a popular song from my youth called "Fools Rush In." The boy's car had fallen in first, and the jeep had come along and fallen into the same trap.

Job 18:10 "The snare is laid for him in the ground, and a trap for him in the way."

Chapter 18. **Be Sure Your Sin Will Find You Out**

It was a dark, cold and rainy day. I wanted to hurry and get through decking some trucks and go home. I was about halfway finished working when a slow driver was getting on my nerves. I decided I might as well use this opportunity to witness to him. The other truck drivers told me that this man was financially secure and didn't need to work much longer. For this and other reasons, the other guys seemed to resent him. However, the man apparently thought a lot of himself because he took about five minutes to tell me that he was a church member and very religious.

Just as soon as he got through telling me what a good guy he was, he turned around and started toward the back of the truck. It was dark, and there was a 4' x 6' oak board lying on the ground where he had placed it. He stumbled over it and fell down on the ground. The oak board got one of the worst cursings anyone has ever heard, as he used the Lord's name in vain. The sad part is, he had religion but not Christ. The scripture says you must be born again.

James 3:11 "Doth a fountain send forth at the same place sweet water and bitter?"

Chapter 19. **The Euclid and the Engineer**

Gene Bradley, who operated a wrecker service in Winston-Salem, called me to come to a rock quarry behind his house and help him recover a Euclid dump truck that had slipped off a dam with the back part submerged in the water. Mr. Bradley had three Mack wreckers, but there was room for only one wrecker on the dam to work the recovery. When I arrived at the scene, I backed up to the front of the big Euclid, got out my snatch blocks and started rigging. There was one tree in a low spot which I could anchor to.

About this time, a man came up to me and told me that he was an engineer with the company which owned the Euclid. He advised me that I didn't need to double back three times because I had more power than I needed. I informed him that I had my own way of doing things, and because of experience, I had to do what I knew was right. I also explained to him that the cables were going to pull hard, and that he should step back because it could be dangerous and I did not want him to get hurt.

I was on top of the dam, so I put Mr. Bradley with one of his wreckers on the ground below me. I used some long cables to shim with by way of a snatch block to another tree back to the bed of the Euclid to keep it from turning over as I winched it out. I was using three five-eighths inch chains at the front of the dump truck. I started winching, and I told Mr. Bradley to keep his line tight and go with the flow. The big tree I anchored to was starting to come out of the ground, but my anchor held. It pulled harder than I thought it would. The Euclid started moving just as I planned. All of a sudden, one of the chains broke. I put all my rigging back in place and doubled back one more time to another tree. This time the Euclid moved, pushing dirt in front of it about two feet high. Success! I proved my point to the engineer.

If I had listened to him, I could have broken a cable and then I would have had to repair it. Mr. Bradley was happy, the helpers were happy, and I was happy. However, I wasn't sure if the engineer was happy. I always have the greatest engineer with me, the Lord Jesus Christ, who is all-powerful.

Psalm 145:11 "They shall speak of the glory of thy kingdom, and talk of thy power...."

Chapter 20. The Disease

This story describes what all wrecker men have experienced. I encountered this problem so often in my career that I gave it a name.

I had just gotten back from Charlotte after winching an Eastern Airlines 727 back on the main runway after its right landing gear had mired up in the snow and mud. A friend of mine, an old electrician, had driven up into a lot on Main Street in Kernersville, and the right front wheel on his truck had fallen into a hole. He came over and asked me if I could lift it out with my wrecker. I told him I would help him out, but I didn't need a wrecker to do the job. I decided to take some oak blocks and a bumper jack to jack up his truck and save him some money.

Just as I started to work, a store owner came over and proceeded to tell me how to get the truck out. I decided that I would go along with him and asked him what I should do. He told me where to put my blocks. I asked him if I should jack up the truck or wait for his instructions. He never answered me and quickly became tired and sweaty because it was 90 degrees in the shade. The oak blocks were heavy, and he was an elderly man who may have never done any hard work with his hands. Sure enough, he did what I expected and said, "Robert, I've got to get back to the store." His way was not working, and he had the "disease" that most sidewalk superintendents have: they try to interfere with a wrecker man's job.

There are three things that are important to remember about sidewalk superintendents. First, they get in the way; second, they get a wrecker man's mind off his business; third, he may hesitate between two opinions. My advice is to stay on track and go with your experience.

James 1:8 "A double minded man is unstable in all his ways."

Chapter 21. **The Winston Lake Job**

This is one of my favorite stories for several reasons: this job included the most rigging; one of my competitors had attempted the job, but failed; and it reminded me of an Old Testament story about the Lord and Moses.

The call came in from the Winston-Salem Street Department saying that Winston Lake had been drained and that a large Link-belt dragline, nicknamed "Big Red," had slipped off a platform into the muck. They needed me to take a look at it. When someone wanted me to look at a job in advance, I knew that it was probably going to be difficult or unusual. When I went to look at the job, I realized why they wanted me to look over the situation first. "Big Red" had backed off the platform with its large boom sideways. I noticed that the front of the tracks were still on the platform, but the machine was reared up, which meant it would be a hard pull. I told them I would give it a try if they would be responsible for the insurance involved. They agreed. I also told them I would be there early the next morning. I asked them to cut a big log from a pine tree that would help raise the front end of the trackhoe and give us leverage.

I went home pondering the situation and realized it would require all the snatch blocks I had to do this particular job. I called a friend of mine to go along with me. That evening, I received a call to winch out a beer truck behind a bar in Kernersville. (It turned out that I had a harder time with the beer truck than the big job the next day.)

When my friend and I arrived the next morning, I backed into the scene and contemplated my strategy. Several things immediately began to happen. When my helper got out of the wrecker, he mired up almost to his waist in the mud. He weighed about 260 pounds. We didn't realize that the lake bed was so rotten. We noticed that when the operator of the dragline backed it off the platform, he had left it in gear. Therefore, we had to take the tracks loose which meant a "dead hard pull." The Lord was always with me, and I had learned when I got out of the way and let the Lord take over, I experienced great confidence that came from studying His word for many years. (I John 5:14 says: "And this is the confidence that we have in Him, that, if we ask anything according to His will, He heareth us.") I realized I had many other things working for me: two bulldozers I could use, a front-end loader and a big log. I sent a boy over to John Yarbrough's Transfer Company to borrow a big clevis because I needed an extra one. John told the boy, "If Robert breaks it, he can have it!" (Actually, he gave me the clevis later.)

Now I will explain how I executed the rigging. After backing up about 40 feet in front of "Big Red," I put one bulldozer on each side with their blades in the ground for a strong anchor. Then I put the front-end loader in front of my wrecker and started rigging to the bulldozers and to the pintle hook behind the wrecker. In all, I doubled back eight times. Being afraid the winch would pull the pintle hook off of "Big Red," I hooked to several places on the rig and also hooked my boom and a nylon band across the top. One more snatch block was needed, and the street department was kind enough to go to their shop and bring me one.

While we were waiting, the young boy whom I had sent to get the big clevis said he thought we needed an air wand. He was beginning to get interested in wreckers and had read about the wand in *Tow Times* magazine. I told him I didn't need a wand, but I did need him to assist my helper in shoveling the mud. I would rather have a good shoveler than an air wand any day.

I put all four of my scotches out and tied them off to the back of the wrecker. I usually left the brakes off until I pulled against the scotches. Then I told the head mechanic I needed him to signal to me just as soon as "Big Red" moved, so I would know how hard I was pulling. I didn't realize until later I told him to signal me by smiling and circling his hand quickly if it started moving, and I would pour the steam to it. I put it in third gear. As the cables tightened, I noticed several sidewalk superintendents, police cars, town officials and observers on the bank watching me. That was when the critical moment arrived. It was during these exciting times that my faith was put to the test, and I gave the Lord all the glory for what was going to be accomplished. "And now for...the rest of the story," as Paul Harvey, a well known radio broadcaster of the twentieth century, was famous for saying.

I truly believed that "Big Red" would emerge from the mud. I checked all the hooks and started pulling. The cables strained. I looked over at the smiling mechanic, and sure enough, his hand was in the air circling quickly, like I asked him to do. I poured the gas to it and "Big Red" started moving. I pulled it until all my snatch blocks came together. That meant I just about had it back on the platform and out of the miry clay. I needed to pull up about 20 more feet and re-rig for the last pull. I asked the supervisor of the job if he would get me a cold Dr. Pepper. He said this was the first time he had seen "Big Red" move after more than a week of trying to get it out. He was so elated that he told me he didn't have a Dr. Pepper, but he would get me some champagne! After "Big Red" was out, the mechanic told me that his arm was killing him from holding it up so long, but he didn't want to let me down.

This job reminded me of the Old Testament story of Moses, where as long as Aaron and Hur held up Moses' hands and staff, the Lord was with Moses. The Lord was certainly with me that day. I was so busy that I forgot to put on the brakes. None of us saw the angels on the other side pushing, but I knew they were there. Two of the head men told me they were going to take me to lunch, and while we were gone, their men would wash all the mud off of my equipment. As I witnessed to them about my Lord and how he had saved me, they both told me they went to church. My prayer was that they had Christ instead of religion.

Exodus 17:11-12 *"And it came to pass, when Moses held up his hand, that Israel prevailed..."*

Chapter 22. **The Horn Blower**

It was a miserable, cold and rainy day. I had just left Beck's Frame and Alignment Shop in Kernersville after lifting up a loaded trailer that had sunk down into the ground. The landing gears were half buried. I was tired, hungry and freezing. The yellow rain suit I was wearing did not breathe. When I became cold and sweaty, I soon cooled off, causing the rain suit to become like a thermos jug; therefore, I got even colder. That was the way I felt when I started back to our shop in town.

On my way to the shop, a ten-speed bike passed me. I knew my Sterling was slow, but I didn't really like being passed by a bicycle! As I got close to the town square, I heard a horn blowing repeatedly behind me. The driver could not possibly know how his anger affected me at this point in time. I wondered how I was going to handle this guy. The scripture verse that says, "Wherefore, my beloved brethren, let every man be swift to hear, slow to speak, slow to wrath…" came to mind, and I decided to test it in an unusual way. I parked my wrecker on the side of the street at the intersection of Main and Mountain Streets. I got out of the wrecker and used a red flag, which I kept in the seat of the cab, to block the intersection both ways. I walked back to the car that was doing all the horn blowing. I tapped on the window, and the driver rolled the window down. I told him I had the intersection completely blocked off for him. I told him I was sorry that my wrecker was so slow, but he could go around me. Much to my surprise he said, "Thank you." What else could he say? I believe the reason he did not get angry was because I went overboard for him, so he could get through traffic without any problem. This verse proved to be true and eliminated my frustration. (I didn't tell him that I had no authority to block the intersection!)

This incident reminded me of how Mr. John Musten Sr., a family friend, who ran Musten and Crutchfield Grocery in Kernersville, would run from his grocery store with his apron on to block the intersection for the volunteer fire department. He also had no authority to block the intersection. He was just a good citizen.

Proverbs 14:29 "He that is slow to wrath is of great understanding: but he that is hasty of spirit exalteth folly."

Chapter 23. **Dead and Gone**

The call came in from Roadway Express that a tractor and trailer had rolled over at old Highway 311 in Horneytown near High Point. The rig had turned over at the edge of a cemetery and was loaded with 48,000 pounds of a liquid chemical in 55 gallon barrels.

The shop manager wanted to know if I could turn the rig back up without unloading it. The tractor and trailer was in a ditch, and unloading the 55 gallon barrels would obviously be impractical in this location. I told him if he would keep the highway patrolman and sidewalk superintendents away from me, I would be able to keep my mind on my business, and I would give it my best try.

When I arrived on the scene, I saw two trees directly across from the big rig which were not very large, but I felt that if I could anchor to both of them, it would greatly assist me in rigging.

I knew that the Lord would be with me. I always looked for something to anchor to, and I liked to think by faith that He had put those trees there just for me. After all, the Hebrew epistle defines faith as "the substance of things hoped for, the evidence of things not seen" (Hebrews: 11:1). I started rigging and doubled back five times via the two trees. I positioned the Sterling at an angle so that when the trees helped to bring the rig up, I would be in the right place to winch it forward since I only had one wrecker. Everything was working just as I had planned. The rig was coming up nicely, but two things worried me: would my anchors hold and would my hook pull out of the hole in the fifth wheel plate?

This was the most critical time. I asked the shop manager if he would be willing to get in the truck and crank it up to build up the air pressure, so we could release the brakes. I then asked the garage operations manager if he would help me pull the cable out of the boom since the big snatch block weighed 100 pounds. Since he had a sport coat and tie on, I didn't know if he would want to help out or not. However, he agreed, so I gave him a pair of gloves and put him to work.

After this final hook up, I started pulling with the boom winch, and at the same time, I kept the rig from turning over with the drag winch. Everything worked perfectly, and the rig came out on the highway. The shop manager drove the rig back to Roadway, put a mirror on the right door, washed it and sent it up the road. The anchors held and there was no damage! I found out later that a patrolman had made a bet that I would not turn the rig up loaded that day. He probably did not know that I was relying on the One who was my real anchor behind the scene, the Lord Jesus Christ.

I came by the cemetery about a year later, and noticed that one of the trees I had anchored to was dead, and the other was gone! Immediately, I thought about how we all will end up in this place when we die. Where you will spend eternity depends on whether or not you have accepted the Lord Jesus Christ as your personal Savior. For a Christian, absent from the body is present with the Lord!

John 3:16 "For God so loved the world, that he gave his only begotten Son, that whosoever believeth in him should not perish, but have everlasting life."

Chapter 24. **Answer to Prayer**

It was a Friday night, and it had been a particularly hard day. I had two new tractors to undeck at Roadway Express. I was about to set the second tractor down when Roadway told me they needed me to go to Highway 158 and switch out a tractor because a driver had broken down with part of the trailer sticking out in the road. I felt that I needed to hurry because someone might come along and clip him. I set the second tractor down and rushed home to get my other wrecker. Anyone who is a wrecker operator with experience switching a tractor out on a busy highway would know that things can get terribly hectic. Everything went smoothly with this call, and I headed home, thinking about the delicious supper Becky would have waiting for me.

Just as I sat down to eat, my pager went off again. This time, I had to go to Greensboro to switch out a tractor which had broken down right before I-40 split with I-85. I knew the exact location of the tractor. It was close to a bridge which was dangerous. Night had set in and it was raining. When I arrived with the replacement tractor, the driver had just passed the bridge and was on the shoulder of the road. The bridge was on a slight curve, and cars were coming around at a fast speed. It reminded me of race cars on a NASCAR track approaching me.

I got the driver to go with me in the wrecker to the next exit. Then, I unhooked the replacement tractor and let him drive it back, so he would be ready to back under the trailer when I pulled the disabled tractor out. Everything was going well, with the exception of a tractor and trailer almost hitting us and running over a triangular flare. As the driver backed under the trailer, I went to help him and told him to hook up the lights first, so the traffic could see the tractor and trailer in the dark. (I had put two magnetic lights on the left rear of the trailer until he could get his lights hooked up.) He informed me he would take care of the lights as soon as he put the landing gears up. I felt he should have taken care of the lights first for safety reasons.

I instructed the driver to go as fast as he could when he started out because he had two pup trailers, and traffic was coming around the curve toward us at least 70 mph. I started back to get the flares up and retrieve the lights I had put on the trailer. However, the driver chose to start out before I got back to the rear of the trailer. Unbelievable! There he went with my lights on the left side, flashing alternately. Immediately, I called the truck shop to see if they could get in touch with him since I was afraid that the lights might fall off or cause a wreck. Being concerned that I might cause someone to get hurt, I asked the Lord to look after me and the driver who had just left. Then I took the tractor to a shopping center nearby and unhooked it, rehooked from the rear and headed back to the tractor shop. All the way back, I was apprehensive about the driver and the lights, and I told the Lord it was up to Him now as it was out of my hands.

The next morning about 11:30, I was playing with my grandchildren when my pager went off. It was the truck shop at Roadway. A new supervisor was on duty, and he asked me if I had left two lights on the back of a tractor and trailer. I told him I had, but I was concerned about what he might say. He said, "A driver came by and brought your two lights back to the shop." He also told me that I was lucky because it was rare for a driver to take the time to bring them back. He didn't know it, but I knew it was a perfect answer to my prayer. The Lord has answered my prayers many times, and I always thank Him. In Luke 17:16, only one of the ten lepers came back to thank Him.

In the gospel of Matthew, the story tells of a leper who came to the Lord and worshiped Him before He healed him. The real lesson of prayer to my mind is this: not only does the Lord hear prayer, but it allows me to worship Him.

Psalm 95:6 "O come, let us worship and bow down: let us kneel before the Lord our maker."

Chapter 25. **The Load of Pigs**

It was a terribly hot day in August. I was listening to the police scanner when a call came in that a tractor and trailer had overturned while carrying a load of pigs. The policeman calling in to the station said in an excited voice, "Send me some help right away—there are pigs everywhere!" At first, I thought I was hearing things, but after the police called me to do the job, it was beginning to make sense.

I arrived at the scene on Business I-40 near the Highway 66 exit at Kernersville. A policeman was in the middle of the interstate trying to herd the pigs back to the overturned tractor and trailer—an impossible task! The policeman had to double as a cowboy that day.

A decision had to be made quickly. The trailer was an aluminum double-decker which made it harder to turn up loaded. The pigs were large, weighing about 400 pounds each and were on top of each other. Many were killed in the accident. I started rigging, doubled back four times and began to turn up the tractor and trailer. If I could turn the rig up without destroying the trailer, it would alleviate the congestion inside the trailer and we would be able to open the rear doors easier.

I started winching and soon determined that this approach would not work. I pulled extremely hard, and my wrecker was being pulled back over the scotches. I was afraid the trailer would split apart. (This was years before the sturdy nylon bands came along.) Meanwhile, the company had several small cattle trailers en route to unload the trailer. When the trailers arrived, we opened one of the doors and began to unload the trailer.

We were wondering whether or not to spray the pigs with water to cool them off with the hose from the fire truck on the scene. I decided to tell the fireman to spray the pigs with water so that more might be saved. Since I was Kernersville's second fire chief, I thought this was feasible. We hoped that some of the pigs were saved.

I was playing golf a few months later with a friend of mine who worked at a meat market in Kernersville. The subject of the pigs came up. He told me the decision to spray them with water was the worst possible choice. He thought this would be fatal to the pigs. At a later time, I discussed this job with a man who raised pigs, and he told me that spraying the pigs with water was not harmful to them. I later heard the testimony of a Christian colonel in the Army stationed at the Pentagon when terrorists flew a plane into the Pentagon in 2001. He stated he was burned over 60 percent of his body and that sprinklers in the building had saved lots of lives that day. The water from the sprinklers poured on his body and saved his life. You decide! To water or not to water? We have to make many decisions in life, but the most important decision that we will ever make is where we will spend eternity. Are you saved or lost? Will you spend eternity in heaven or hell?

John 3:36 "He that believeth on the Son hath everlasting life: and he that believeth not the Son shall not see life; but the wrath of God abideth on him."

Snapshots: A Look Back

SNAPSHOTS: A LOOK BACK

The Sterling as it was when purchased in 1947.
From left: Ned R. Stuart, Sr., Ned R. Stuart, Jr. and Robert Stuart.

Father and son, a great team.
Highway 29 between Greensboro and Reidsville, N.C. (1960).

"Saved By the Rock" in Fancy Gap, Virginia.

A loaded tractor and trailer overturned with a fatality.

Mr. Walt Idol, a faithful helper, overseeing a
tractor and trailer being uprighted.

Robert removing a grease rack at a service station (1952).

Robert recovering a load of liquid rubber.

Setting a 13,000 lb. steel boiler at Kernersville School.

A 727 recovered from snow and mud at Douglas Airport in Charlotte, N.C.

A Whisper Jet being winched back on the runway at
Piedmont Triad International Airport in Greensboro, N.C.

A nighttime recovery of another Whisper Jet in Greensboro.

"Big Red" at Winston Lake.

Rigging "Big Red."

"Big Red" recovered.

Uprighting a modular office.

A loaded earthmover recovered.

A cliffhanger: the trailer, loaded with 28,000 lbs. of wool, dangles above the frozen Yadkin River at Spencer, N.C.

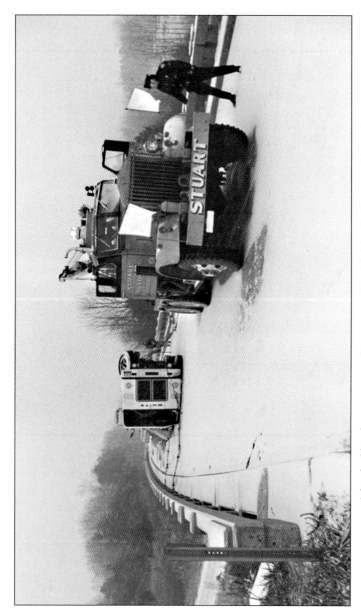

A load of lumber overturned on an overhead bridge in Kernersville, N.C.

Catch of the Day! Two at a time at Kernersville Lake bridge.

Robert and long-time friend, Bruce Kirkman,
after removing a cement mixer bowl.

Moving a Masonic Temple (1947).

Overturned tanker loaded with liquid grease in Kernersville, N.C.

Son, Russ, unloading jiff locks (1986).

Robert and Russ after completing the job.

Recovering a gas tanker in Thomasville, N.C.

Switching engines on a helicopter.

Chapter 26. **The Perfect Mattress**

A call came in about 5:00 one morning and woke me up. An officer from the High Point Police Department was on the other end of the line telling me a loaded tanker containing milk had overturned at Highway 311 southbound approaching High Point. I called Kenny Crews, a friend of mine, to go with me and drive my Autocar. When we arrived, the tanker, a straight truck, had flipped over on its top. This truck had a stainless steel tank with a full load of milk weighing approximately 60,000 pounds. Milk was leaking out of the main hatch. I had to make a quick decision. There was no one to pump the milk out of the tank. Would the tank burst when I turned it up? I decided to go for it.

I put the Sterling in all-wheel drive and started down the slope of the road to get in the correct position to turn the tanker up. Another friend of mine, who lived nearby, was watching the recovery and offered to help us. I sent him to a garage in Kernersville where I had stored three mattresses that came out of a sleeper just for this type of situation. This would be the first time I had used a mattress on a job. I placed the mattresses in position for the wheels to come down on them for a soft landing. Bear in mind, there were no springs but a soft, thick surface. There was no place to put a chain over the chassis because the bottom of the tank was flush with the top of the frame. I improvised by taking one-half inch chains and crisscrossed them tightly with two load binders, spring hanger to spring hanger. This gave me a good place to put my snatch blocks at the highest point of the rigging.

As I was winching the tanker, it started sliding toward me. The tires would not dig into the road. I took my Autocar wrecker and anchored low on the other side. This strategy worked well. At this juncture, I stopped. I told Kenny which signals to use and to let me know how the other side of the tanker was doing. He was standing at the rear telling me to go ahead. I was glad that I had turned everything over to the Lord. I did not know for sure whether or not the tanker would burst and spew milk everywhere or if my mattresses would work as I had planned. The tanker was coming down slowly at first, and then it seemed to pick up speed. I held my breath. It was in the Lord's hands. When it landed on the mattresses, the entire tanker bounced up off the ground. It leaned toward me a little and then set down perfectly on my mattresses. I looked over at Kenny at the end of the tanker. His eyes were as big as golf balls! Success!

Deuteronomy 25:15 "But thou shalt have a perfect and just weight..."

Chapter 27. **Wrecker Not Required**

A friend of mine, who was the head man at a construction company, called and explained that he had a backhoe stuck in Lake Lassiter, a drained lake in Winston-Salem. He asked, "Can you bring your tools and recover it for us? A wrecker cannot get to it, but we have a bulldozer with a winch on the back near the backhoe." He sent a pickup truck to get me and my equipment: snatch blocks, chains, clevises and 30 feet of seven-eighths and three-fourths inch slings. Many rigging possibilities presented themselves because when I got there, there were two bulldozers instead of one.

It was going to be a joy to get in this muddy mess for many reasons. First, it was a real challenge. Second, there was no pressure from a blocked road. Third, there was no patrolman asking me how long it would take. Fourth, the construction crew could not turn into sidewalk superintendents because they had no idea how to string cables to the bulldozers which I used for portable anchors. Last but not least, I could move my anchors wherever I needed them.

I took my time, and everything worked just as I planned with one exception—cleaning up my equipment and myself was a job in itself. (In the same way, I never thought I played a good game of football unless I got my face scratched and full of mud. We did not have nose guards in those days. I also believed that if I played aggressively, I would not get blindsided or hurt.) On that day, I had no wrecker, but I had the Lord with me...and He is with me forever. This always makes for a great game plan!

John 15:4 "Abide in me, and I in you. As the branch cannot bear fruit of itself, except it abide in the vine; no more can ye, except ye abide in me."

Chapter 28. **The Red Heifer**

After lunch one day, I thought I would work out in the yard, but as usual, the phone rang with an unusual request and interrupted my plans. My dear friend, Leo Whicker, asked me to come to his farm to pull one of his cows out of a muddy, swamp-like part of his pasture which was loaded with piles of manure and numerous uneven knolls. Sure enough, one of his red heifer cows was stuck in the mud up to her neck. There were some additional problems. Leo had a rope around the cow's neck that was too small, not strong enough and would probably cut into the neck of the cow with a strong pull from my wrecker. Leo had to get down into the mud with his cow to hold its head up out of the mud. This allowed the cow to breathe and prevented it from taking a nose dive when I pulled it out, which would have created a worse situation.

I took my big Sterling wrecker because the boom was higher than my Autocar, and I could make the winch move more rapidly in overdrive. We got hooked up, and I replaced the rope with a wide nylon band around the cow's neck to keep it from cutting or hurting the cow. I put the wrecker in third gear and at the signal from Leo, I started to pull. As we moved about 10 feet, Leo let the cow's nose go down into the mud. I stopped while Leo dug her head out of the mud and we started a second time. I put the wrecker in overdrive and "poured the coal" to it. I raced the motor and out came Leo and the red heifer traveling at a speed of about 10 mph. Success at last! This was probably the fastest the cow had ever moved around in the pasture! As soon as she came out of the mud on dry ground, we unhooked her. She got up and instinctively went straight to her calf. The mother, the calf, Leo and I were all satisfied. There were no injuries or harm to the cow.

The red heifer in the Old Testament was used in purification ceremonies for the removal of sin. The Lord Jesus sacrificed himself by dying on the cross for sinners; therefore, the red heifer is symbolic of Christ.

Numbers 19:2 "This is the ordinance of the law which the Lord hath commanded, saying, Speak unto the children of Israel, that they bring thee a red heifer without spot, wherein is no blemish, and upon which never came yoke..."

Chapter 29. **The Hand Car**

I was in Winston-Salem one day moving a large 10,000 gallon tank which was quite close to a train track. I had to be careful when I lifted the tank off the ground because I had to operate on an uneven surface. I had to extend the boom on the wrecker all the way out so it would be high enough to be in a center position because the tank was so large. When I lifted the tank, it moved too close to the railroad. It was close enough to hit a train if one came down the track.

I was always careful to practice safety; however, in this case, I made a big mistake which could have been a fatal mistake. I did not take the time to put out the dead legs on the wrecker to keep it level. I knew better, but I thought I could keep the tank away from the tracks. I sent a man up the tracks with a red flag to warn a train in case one was approaching. Looking back on the situation, it was ridiculous to send a man up the tracks thinking this would stop a train in time. I meant well, but meaning well does not always solve the problem.

When the tank cleared the ground, it went left and set down on the railroad ties next to the rails. All of the wheels on the right side of the wrecker were off the ground. Just at this time, the man I sent up the track came running back yelling that a train was coming! I panicked and let the tank down to take the weight off, put the wrecker in all-wheel drive and low range. I tried to move the tank away from the tracks. I remember exactly what I said at this time, "Oh, please Lord, no!" All of a sudden, a hand car came down the track and stopped! I do not think I have seen a hand car since. (A hand car is a four-wheel vehicle that takes two men to operate and it is used to inspect the rails on a train track.) The man with the red flag mistakenly thought the hand car was a train. Isn't the Lord good? Just don't get yourself in a bad situation to start with!

Ecclesiastes 7:17 "Be not over much wicked, neither be thou foolish: why shouldest thou die before thy time?"

Chapter 30. **The Green Sweater**

My daughter probably would have a hard time believing that I would write this chapter about the green sweater, as we always laughed about its absurdity.

Although this incident occurred many years ago, I remember it well. It was during the time the construction of I-40 from Kernersville to Winston-Salem had started, and congestion was everywhere. Construction vehicles crisscrossed the road at times, and it made travel very dangerous. My dad was in the hospital recovering from a stroke, and I was on my way back to Kernersville after visiting him when a call came in to go to an accident on I-40. I did not have time to change clothes, so I jumped in the wrecker and started to the scene.

When I arrived at the scene, I felt a strong urge to go to the bathroom, and there was no holding this off. This is every wrecker man's nightmare! I walked up and over an embankment, and as I finished, I realized I had no toilet paper with me. I didn't know what in the world I was going to do. I had just purchased a brand new green polyester sweater. I had no other choice but to use it, and I thanked the Lord I had the sweater with me that day. It was the best toilet paper that I have every used. Always be prepared for unexpected emergencies!

I Thessalonians 5:18 "In everything give thanks: for this is the will of God in Christ Jesus concerning you."

Chapter 31. The $21 Million Job

The telephone rang about 1:00 a.m. A highway patrolman said a moving van had turned over down an embankment on Highway 29-70 in Greensboro. He wanted me to come over and look at the job and tell him if I could turn up and winch the rig out without unloading it. He said if I could not turn it up loaded, then I would have to wait until morning for the FBI to supervise the unloading before I could start work. This was a mystery to me. What could the trailer be loaded with and why would the FBI be involved? I got in my 1940 Ford and took off to check it out. When I arrived, the first person I met was the patrolman. I asked him what the trailer contained. He told me that the trailer was loaded with priceless furnishings from the Turkish embassy that were insured for $21 million. That solved the mystery! I went back to Kernersville to get my Sterling wrecker and called Charlie Barnard to go with me.

The load was not very heavy, and I thought I could easily pull it up the bank. I positioned my wrecker at an angle, so when I turned up the van, I would still be in a position to hold it and winch it up the embankment. Just as I got the van up the bank and started out on the road, a battery cable on the van shorted and started smoking. I used a small fire extinguisher to put out the fire, and I knew I was home free. After evaluating this job, one thing stood out: no one had asked me how much insurance I had. The patrolman told me later that his troop commander was bragging about the largest insured wreck he had ever worked, which was about $3 million. The patrolman told him that was nothing, and he worked a job once which was insured for $21 million. The commander thought the patrolman was pulling his leg.

Ephesians 3:3-5 "How that by revelation he made known unto me the mystery; (as I wrote afore in few words, Whereby, when ye read, ye may understand my knowledge in the mystery of Christ) Which in other ages was not made known unto the sons of men, as it is now revealed unto his holy apostles and prophets by the Spirit..."

Chapter 32. **Asleep In the Cockpit**

Several years ago before Eastern Airlines went out of business, I pulled eight of their airplanes out of the mud and back on the runway. I went to the Greensboro Airport five times and Douglas Airport in Charlotte three times. It would take me about four hours to get to Charlotte going 40 mph in my Sterling wrecker.

Eastern Airlines called me on a snowy morning about 4:00 to come to the Douglas Airport. A 727 had the main runway blocked with one landing gear off in the snow and mud. Because of the weather, the pilot had missed the turn, and the plane was mired up to the axle. I informed the maintenance manager on the phone that it was snowing in Kernersville, and it would take me longer to get there with my wrecker, but I would head that way. He thanked me and said if they got the plane out before I arrived, they would still pay me for my time. Since the manager respected me enough to treat me in this manner, I suppose I would have gone anywhere he asked. I didn't know it at the time, but this was the last job I would do for Eastern because they later went out of business.

I called Ronnie McKnight, one of my loyal helpers, to go with me. We put a spare tire on the back of the wrecker and left immediately. After driving in the snow for most of the night, we finally arrived in Charlotte. The crew on the scene was happy to see us and treated us to breakfast before we started working. It was a privilege to work for a great company like Eastern.

After breakfast, we went out to the main runway to the 727. Eastern had a large tug that weighed around 50,000 pounds. I had the driver move the tug off the runway into the mud, so I could use it for an anchor. I started rigging as follows: I doubled back to the tug two times, and from there, I doubled back three times from the back of the wrecker to the airplane. I hooked two three-fourths inch slings together from the landing gear back to a certain point, so I would not put out too much cable off my big wrecker. The first pull brought the plane back about 10 feet, and then the three-fourths inch cable broke. Although the plane moved back, two unexpected things happened: the right wing tilted closer to the ground, and mud and snow built up about three feet in front of the plane's landing gears. An airport runway is one of the coldest places you can be in the winter; therefore, it was difficult for Ronnie and me to shovel into the deep, frozen mud and snow for our cribbing under the landing gear. Consequently, someone with Eastern would say, "Let's try it again." The maintenance crew assisted us in the shoveling.

After rigging again, we tried winching as before, and this time the same thing happened with the exception that our anchor, the big tug, held. However, the landing gear would not come up, pushing more mud and snow in front of the wheel. Now we had a new problem because the right wing of the plane was getting closer to the ground. The supervisor told us the National Guard had some air bags we could use. As we put them under the wing and started to inflate them, one blew out because the maintenance crew did not stack them properly. As a result, the plane shook violently. Needless to say, our nerves were shaken as well!

We started the procedure again, and this time we were successful! The landing gear rose up out of the way, and we cribbed under it nicely. The landing gear was put back in and locked in place. It was getting late in the evening when we made our last pull.

To give you a better concept of what was happening, picture this: the GPU (ground power unit) was on the right side of me screaming loudly, and I was on the left side of the wrecker with the boom rotated out of the way so that when the plane came out on the runway, it would not hit my wrecker.

Strange things were about to take place. The supervisor told me to start winching at the same time he let the air out of the air bags. He was also communicating with the crew in the cockpit. At this time, reinforcements from Miami had replaced the first maintenance crew. The plane started moving, and everything seemed to be working fine until the two giant wheels of the landing gear finally came up on the runway. The cables, which had been fairly tight, began getting slack. A strong wind caused the plane to pick up speed. It was heading toward me and the GPU! The mechanic at the controls was asleep in the cockpit! The supervisor yelled at the mechanic and woke him up in time for him to put on the brakes.

One of the hardest things to recover is a 150,000 pound airplane with the fuel out. However, once the plane is on the runway, the wind can move it. We need the Lord in our cockpit at all times.

Psalm 121:3-4 "He will not suffer thy foot to be moved: he that keepeth thee will not slumber. Behold, he that keepeth Israel shall neither slumber nor sleep."

Chapter 33. **The Blue Light Special**

It was a cold, rainy morning around 4:00 when I received a call from the High Point Police Department. The dispatcher said they had a tractor and trailer turned over, completely blocking the northbound lane of Highway 29-70. I called Walt Idol to help me, and we left Kernersville in a hurry. A wrecker man's nightmare is a cold, wet morning with an urgent call. When we arrived, there were three small wreckers attempting to turn up the rig. They made a crucial mistake by taking the tractor loose from the fifth wheel. A common occurrence for a wrecker man is that other people make things harder for him.

The first procedure was to lift the tractor off the ground and swing it back into the fifth wheel and lock it. I then began my rigging. Because the trailer was loaded with steel, I doubled back five times, scotched the wheels and started to take up slack. I had almost forgotten the three small wreckers. I positioned them on the opposite side to hook on the underside of the rig.

This would help stabilize the rig since steel was sticking out from a hole in the top of the trailer and made the weight distribution uneven.

I started up with the entire rig, and everything was going well. While I was freezing in the frigid rain and stressed over the "hurry-up" pressure, a sudden, urgent pain hit me. I told Walt that I had to go to the bathroom immediately. Since the rig was two feet off the ground, Walt told me I needed to let the rig back down first, so it would remain stable until I returned. I reversed the winch and started to let the rig down when I heard Walt yelling, "Stop!" He told me that all three small wreckers were raised up in the air with their front ends off the ground! At this point, I stopped and told Walt, "I gotta go!" A nice High Point lieutenant took me to a bathroom in his police car with his red lights flashing. (Years ago, the police used red lights instead of blue.) When I came back to the scene, I finished turning up the tractor and trailer, and the three wreckers on the other side were lowered to the ground. When you see a police car racing to a scene with his blue lights flashing, he might be rescuing an anxious wrecker man in this same predicament. And that is why the blue light may be crucial to a wrecker man some day.

Daniel 6:27 "He delivereth and rescueth, and he worketh signs and wonders in heaven and in earth, who hath delivered Daniel from the power of the lions."

Chapter 34. **Bucky Smith**

The call came in from the Town of Kernersville that they had a loaded garbage truck turned over in a ditch. The driver of the garbage truck was Bucky Smith, who was a friend of mine. When I arrived on the scene, I asked Bucky what caused him to end up in the ditch. He didn't want to tell me at first, but he reluctantly revealed to me that he had turned to look at a girl wearing shorts in a tobacco field—not once, not twice, but three times. Taking your eyes off the road just one time is all that it takes to cause an accident.

I did a study on the book of Proverbs years ago, and I noticed that chapter 4, verse 25 says, "Let thine eyes look right on, and let thine eyelids look straight before thee." If Bucky had applied this verse, he might not have ended up in the ditch. Fortunately, no one was injured, and no damage was done to the garbage truck. This is a great lesson to all of us.

II Timothy 3:16 *"All scripture is given by inspiration of God, and is profitable for doctrine, for reproof, for correction, for instruction in righteousness..."*

Chapter 35. **How Much Cable?**

One of my customers called and said he had a tractor and trailer loaded with steel turned over in a ditch near East Forsyth High School in Kernersville. I called two of my helpers and asked them to meet me at the scene and bring my Autocar since I would be driving the Sterling. When I arrived, I started looking for some trees to anchor to, and sure enough, the Lord had placed several trees in the perfect location where I needed them, right across from the overturned rig. I began my rigging and doubled back five times using two of the trees. I placed the Autocar in front and put the Sterling in a catty-cornered position, so the trees would take the hardest pull, and I would be in a position to winch the rig up the road when it came over. Everything went according to plan, and the tractor and trailer came over and out in the same rigging. I had a lot of cable out and was winding it in when a man came up and asked me this question, "Stuart, how many feet of cable did you use on this job?" I was in a good mood because the stress was over and the job was a success. I answered without hesitation, "I used 535 feet." I didn't have time to count how many feet of cable I used on a job. However, I was always amazed at questions I was asked at a wreck scene, so sometimes I gave amazing answers! We checked the oil level, and the driver cranked up the engine and drove off.

Luke 21:14 "Settle it therefore in your hearts, not to meditate before what ye shall answer..."

Chapter 36. **Never Do It**

A call came in one Sunday morning from Roadway Express that a tractor and trailer had overturned in the median at Linville Road and Business 40. The dispatcher informed me that it was loaded with 55,000 pounds of short pieces of wood which were stacked on pallets. I called Ronnie McKnight, who helped me when I needed him, to bring the Autocar and meet me there.

When I arrived with the Sterling, I asked the manager in charge of the job what condition the load was in, and he told me that he did not think the load had shifted because it was very compact. He also wanted me to turn the rig up loaded. On a previous job in High Point, I turned up a load of 55 gallon barrels of a liquid substance that weighed about 48,000 pounds with no damage. I told him that I would attempt it if he would not let anyone bother me or pressure me in any way, especially a state trooper. Since the manager was also present at the High Point job and was very helpful, I agreed to try to lift up the loaded trailer. It would be a real mess to unload.

I started my rigging. I doubled back five times with my last hook up to the fifth wheel plate. The plates had gotten thinner over the years, but I had a special chain that I used in the holes. I remember one time that the hook I was using had cut through the fifth wheel plate on a trailer like a knife through butter. I positioned my Autocar up the road where it would be in the perfect position to winch the rig out when I raised it up. If it came up nicely,

Ronnie had to be prepared to winch it out as soon as possible because something could pull loose at this critical stage. The ditch in the median would probably not let the rig set down evenly, and it would have a tendency to go back over. I always paused to tell the Lord I needed Him. I asked Him to be with me on His day, and I would give Him all the glory. After all, this was His day, Sunday. With everything ready, I started winching. The trailer began to come up. It was always a thrill to me to think that angels were on the other side pushing. It set down quite well, just as I knew it would; but as I suspected, it had a tendency to go back over.

An old friend of mine, Moir Whicker, was parked across the access road at a motel watching me. I was just about to tell Ronnie to start winching when Moir yelled out to me, "You will never do it!" I could have choked him! I looked over, and when I saw Moir, I ignored him. (You can be sure that we laughed about this later.) When the cables on the Autocar tightened, I kept a slight pull to help Ronnie because I was afraid something would come loose if I pulled any harder. I had all the brakes loose on the rig, and I scotched the wheels on the tractor to keep it from rolling back. The tractor and trailer came out as planned. We checked the oil, cranked it up and drove off. There was no damage!

The Lord was with me again, as He has been all these years. The head manager at Roadway Express called me some months later and wanted me to go to Marion to work another wreck. I turned him down because it was too far for me to go in the Sterling at 40 mph. He told me later that a safety man, who was with the manager the day I had turned up the loaded trailer in Kernersville, decided to let another wrecker service in Marion turn this one up loaded. The manager told him not to try it. They attempted it anyway and tore it all to pieces.

Proverbs 13:13 "Whoso despiseth the word shall be destroyed: but he that feareth the commandment shall be rewarded."

Chapter 37. The Cast and the Cabbage

I was recuperating from a knee operation which involved torn cartilage and pulled ligaments, and I was wearing a full cast on my leg. I was getting the royal treatment and being waited on hand and foot by my wife when the phone rang on a Sunday afternoon. My wife answered the phone. It was a call from the state highway patrol. A tractor and trailer loaded with 38,000 pounds of cabbage was close to turning over on the edge of an embankment.

My dad had gone to the mountains to spend the day. My wife told the trooper that I could not go because I had just had surgery, but she would check with me to see if I could recommend someone else. I was surprised she said I could not go because back in those days, nothing could stop me from going on a big call! I called a good helper, my friend, Chuck Hanner, and he helped me get into the wrecker. We drove to Oak Ridge and Highway 68. Seven hours later, we got the tractor and trailer back on the road. Heaven only knows how many times I walked up and down that embankment. The doctor had previously told me to try to exercise my knee cap in the cast, but I may have over-done it a little that day!

When I got home, my dad made a stink because I broke two five-eighths inch chains during the rigging. My wife discontinued the royal treatment since she thought I could take care of myself. I'll never understand why my dad, wife and doctor were upset with me. I thought I did a nice recovery job on one good leg under the circumstances!

Psalm 147:10-11 "He delighted not in the strength of the horse: he taketh not pleasure in the legs of a man. The Lord taketh pleasure in them that fear him, in those that hope in his mercy."

Chapter 38. **The Confrontation and the Soiled Shirt**

A motor line in Greensboro called me about an accident that happened in Ramseur. It involved one of their tractor and trailers which ended up in a plowed field. Another wrecker service had tried to get it out but was unsuccessful. Someone from Charlotte recommended they call me.

When two of my helpers and I arrived at the scene with my Autocar and Sterling wreckers, the rig looked like it had dropped from the sky into the field. The tractor had separated from the loaded trailer, and the landing gears were in the ground. After surveying the scene, I positioned both wreckers on the road, doubled back four times with the Sterling and once with the Autocar. I started winching and the process was slow, but sure. The landing gears reminded me of a dozer plow because it was so difficult to pull.

A state trooper soon came up to me, telling me that I would have to move off the road because traffic was going to increase in about an hour. After much discussion and trying to reason with him about all the trouble it would be to move all of my rigging from the road into the field, I decided to go to Plan B. I always preferred to stay on high ground rather than get down into the mud. (A good analogy is the "slough of despond" from John Bunyan's *Pilgrim's Progress.* In Bunyan's book, the Christian falls into a deep bog because of the load of his sins, and it was this that the mud reminded me of.) It is tough enough to do a job, but when someone interferes, it makes it twice as hard. After thinking it over, I realized that it might not be such a bad idea to transfer my equipment to the field. This would eliminate the traffic problem and get the trooper out of my way. I began to put Plan B into action. Since I was a young Christian, I knew I had to control my temper. First, I told the trooper that I was a Christian, and I was sorry I had blocked his road. While I was talking with him, I gave him a gentle hug, not realizing that I had placed my greasy hand on the back of his nice clean shirt. This obviously didn't improve his disposition. He also told me that

I would get a bill from the state for tearing up the asphalt with my scotches!

When I got the tractor and trailer out about 4 a.m., I noticed the four marks I had made in the asphalt had been packed down by traffic and were barely noticeable. I didn't receive a bill from the state for the asphalt or for a new shirt. When you honor the Lord and His Word, He looks after you!

Proverbs 15:1 "A soft answer turneth away wrath: but grievous words stir up anger."

Chapter 39. **The Grease Rack**

Our shop, Stuart Motor Company, was located next to a service station. In the 1950s, a service station's grease rack was located outside the station. The grease rack consisted of two I-beams bolted onto a strong base on top of a large piston. There was a hole in the ground with at least six tons of concrete around it. The grease rack needed to be replaced. Some workmen dug around the piston and called my dad to bring the wrecker over to lift it out. Pop told me to try to shake the piston a little to dislodge it, so we could lift it out of the hole. We had just purchased two new five-eighths inch log chains from a company up north. I hooked up the chains and geared the wrecker down in low range and front-wheel drive. I started off, but the chain broke. Pop told me to go get another chain and try it again. This chain also broke. I went back to the shop to retrieve an old chain, and this one did the trick. Sometimes old is better!

Ronald McLean, a good friend who played high school football with me, and who was observing our work that day, told me later that the chains looked like rubber bands stretching before they broke. My dad later wrote a letter to the chain company telling them that their chains had broken. Shortly after, a representative of the chain company came to our shop to inquire how this had happened. I don't think he believed our story, but nevertheless, it was true.

Shortly before this book was published, my friend, Ronald, went home to be with the Lord. I visited him before he passed away, and I had the privilege to speak at his funeral. I cherish the memories we shared.

John 10:35 "...and the scripture cannot be broken..."

Chapter 40. **Take Heed Lest You Fall**

One Saturday evening, a 1955 Chevrolet lost traction and slid sideways into the end of a guardrail. The accident occurred on a long sweeping curve that entered into an overhead bridge approaching Kernersville. Interstate 40 had just been built. The curve was misleading because it was banked incorrectly and caused many accidents. A local highway patrolman came by our shop and informed us that a man was pinned in a car on I-40. The guardrail penetrated the floor board and wrapped around the driver's leg, pinning it like a leg iron. Two small boys were thrown out of the vehicle.

I jumped into the Sterling, rushing to be a big hero. I had quite a surprise waiting on me when I arrived at the scene. I cut across the median, running cars off the road to get to the wreck. The car with the guardrail sticking through it reminded me of a ball of yarn on a long needle. Everything I tried was unsuccessful. It wasn't long until it seemed the Lord impressed on me: "If you think you are so hot, let's see what you are going to do with this situation!" After much distress, we got the driver out. He and the two boys survived. I learned a valuable lesson that day: take heed lest you fall! After that, every time I left the shop I would say to myself, "I am a good rigger and wrecker man, but Lord, you know that I need you every day and that I cannot make it without you one second." Without the Lord, you can do nothing!

John 15:5 "I am the vine, ye are the branches: He that abideth in me, and I in him, the same bringeth forth much fruit: for without me ye can do nothing."

Chapter 41. **Hook To Hook**

It was getting dark one evening, and I had a little more welding to do on the rack that holds all of my snatch blocks on the back of the Sterling. My wife, Becky, paged me and said that I had a call. It seldom failed that a call would come at the most inappropriate time. The driver on the other end of the line explained to me that he had four coils of steel leaning dramatically on an aluminum trailer, weighing 42,000 pounds. That meant that I had to quickly put eight snatch blocks weighing 45 pounds each back on the rack. (The older I got, the heavier the snatch blocks seemed.)

When I arrived at the scene, I saw immediately that the driver had not exaggerated. The coils were in a terrific strain against two three-eighths inch log chains. If one of the chains broke, then the weight could damage the center of the trailer. At first, I didn't notice the real hidden danger in which I was involved. It always pays to "walk around" the job before starting. For some reason, I didn't do that this time, and it just about got me in trouble.

After putting a big strap through the center of the coil and protecting it with a large piece of tire rubber, I started to hook a five-eighths inch chain to the end of the strap when I noticed something I had never seen before. The driver had two three-eighths inch log chains dogged down in an X pattern to his trailer to hold the coils. This was done correctly; however, he had connected two hooks together (hook to hook) instead of in a link. The reason he told me he did it this way was because the chain wasn't long enough. I could hardly believe my eyes! He had no idea how dangerous this was—it could have come loose at any time. Unbelievably, he also told me that the load had shifted when a woman had stopped suddenly in front of him in South Carolina. How he drove it all the way from South Carolina without the hooks coming loose with all of the tension on it was truly a small miracle! I winched the coils of steel back in place, and the driver was ready to go.

This dear truck driver turned out to be a born-again Christian. He told me that he had passed from death to life. He also had "Jesus is Lord" written on the cab of his truck. After I winched the coils back into position, we went to get a cup of coffee and enjoyed about an hour of fellowship. Both of us wholeheartedly agreed that the Lord, in His marvelous grace, looks after His own. We both gave the Lord thanks that day for protecting us.

Psalm 91:1 "He that dwelleth in the secret place of the most High shall abide under the shadow of the Almighty."

Chapter 42. **The Secret Weapon**

It was March, 1960, and snow was falling. This was the second snow of the year, and at the time, I never dreamed it would snow four Wednesdays in a row. Roadway Express had just moved to Kernersville. I received a call from them about a tractor and trailer loaded with 50,000 pounds that had gone off into a deep ditch and was in a leaning position off of Highway 150. When I arrived, the pessimistic driver came up and told me that I would never be able to get him out. Little did he know that I had a secret weapon. I had just designed and made four scotches out of scraper blades. When the scotches worked properly with the weight of the wrecker (41,000 pounds) on top of them, it would take a lot of power to move the wrecker; therefore, the scotches would make a reliable anchor.

I began rigging and doubled back two times and set out my scotches. The first pull dragged the wrecker back. The snow was getting deeper, and I happened to be located at the coldest place in Kernersville. It was becoming even colder, and the weather reminded me of when I was in Alaska. The scotches would not dig in because the ground was frozen as hard as a brick. I anchored to a tractor and trailer that had stopped because of the congested traffic. I pulled once more and slid back again. I needed more weight to anchor to, so I called the foreman at Roadway to send another tractor and trailer for this purpose. Thankfully, an elderly woman came out of her house and brought me a hot cup of coffee before the last pull.

After the third attempt, the rig came out of the ditch. My secret weapon, the four scotches, did not work at all in this situation. When you know the Lord, you really don't need a secret weapon!

Psalm 25:14 "The secret of the Lord is with them that fear him; and he will shew them his covenant."

Chapter 43. **Take This Shovel**

On a beautiful August morning, a tractor and trailer tanker loaded with liquid rubber went off a steep embankment, turned over and separated the tractor from the trailer. The location was between the Sandy Ridge exit and Highway 66 in Kernersville. The tanker had ruptured, and a majority of the load had leaked out into a creek which ran into High Point.

I got the tractor out first and then started to recover the tanker. Since the tanker was on its top, I had to turn it over first, so I could winch it up the embankment using the same rigging.

As I tried to winch the tanker over the precipice, it reminded me of trying to wrestle with a big cigar. I had winched the tanker as far as I could with the center pull as the snatch blocks came together. I had also anchored to a tractor and trailer and a load of lumber nearby. I had painted myself into a corner.

The patrolman on the scene was one of the veteran troopers who would have done anything for me. However, when I asked him to shut down the eastbound lane so I could anchor to another tractor and trailer, he took the pipe out of his mouth and looked bewildered because the westbound lane was already closed. This meant that the entire highway would be blocked. That was the first time I had ever seen him rattled because he was so easy-going, but he agreed to do this for me anyway.

I anchored one more time to a tractor and trailer in the eastbound lane. I had cables in three different directions to keep the "big cigar" stabilized. I had only one more choice: to hook the boom to the front of the tanker to keep it high enough so that the landing gears would clear the ground. The center pull could not be used because I had pulled the snatch blocks together and this put me in a bind. I put the Sterling in four-wheel drive and low range, so I could drive out with it—in other words, manhandle it. The tanker had more liquid left in it than I thought.

The only person I had helping me was Charlie Warren, an 18 year old quarterback for East Forsyth High School. I gave him a shovel and told him to shovel mud out from under all the wheels. About this time, a sidewalk superintendent showed up and said, "Why don't…"—and that's all I let him say. I didn't need to hear his opinion since I had done all I knew to do! I told him, "If you want to help, take this shovel and help Charlie dig." Surprisingly, he followed these instructions without another word. When the shoveling was completed, I got into the wrecker, put it in low range, extra low and all-wheel drive and asked the Lord to help me. The tanker came out on the first try and onto the road. An activity bus was close by, and I got a big cheer from the cheerleaders. Isn't that a great reward for a wrecker man? Absolutely! The Lord was with me that day, and I always give Him the honor and glory for who He is!

John 12:26 "...if any man serve me, him will my father honour."

Chapter 44. The Slickest Night Ever!

A trucking company from Greensboro had a tractor and trailer which had slid off into a ditch in front of the Old Mill of Guilford on Highway 68 in Oak Ridge. This was a very dangerous place because it was at the bottom of two steep hills with two lane traffic. It was about 3:00 in the morning. The temperature was around freezing, and it was misting rain—a precursor to black ice. Charlie Barnard, my old sidekick, went with me and drove his red Ford pickup truck with dual Pep Boy tires on the rear which helped keep the truck on the road. We hooked up the tractor and trailer, taking a chance on the traffic hindering us, and recovered it quickly. I backed the Sterling wrecker onto a dirt road leading to a gradual downhill grade to the Old Mill. The road went straight for about 75 yards and then turned into the mill. An old Ford pickup truck was parked in front of the mill. I set the emergency brake, got out of my wrecker, and wrote out the bill. I never noticed the ground was getting colder and freezing quickly. The mist was like a fine lubricant making the road slicker by the minute.

All of a sudden, Charlie yelled to me and said, "There goes your wrecker!" A chill went up my spine. I wondered what he was talking about, but I soon found out! The heat of the tires broke the friction of them to the ground, and the wrecker started sliding down the road toward the Old Mill and the pickup truck. My heart sank because I was afraid the wrecker would slide back into one of the deep gulleys beside the road. I started to run and catch it, but I soon realized it was useless. We watched in disbelief as the wrecker slid down and followed the curvature of the road. It curved left slightly in front of the mill and headed straight for the pickup. I couldn't have backed it better myself.

The wrecker totaled the pickup and stopped just before it went into the mill. The wrecker's boom hit the canopy in front of the mill and made a deafening noise. This was a blessing in disguise. If the pickup had not been parked in front of the mill, the wrecker would have gone into the mill. A mobile home where the caretaker and his wife lived was close to the mill. They were the owners of the pickup truck. When the noise woke them up, they thought an airplane had crashed from the nearby airport. When they came out, they couldn't believe what had happened but were surprisingly understanding. After I finished this job, I got into the Sterling and drove off. There had been no damage to the wrecker. Believe it or not, this was just the beginning of the slickest night!

By now, we had another call, and Charlie and I left to go to Highway 421. Just as I turned onto the highway, the wrecker made a semicircle because the roads were getting slicker. I had never experienced this before. When I turned the wrecker around, we headed toward Stanleyville to recover another tractor and trailer stuck by the side of the road.

We stopped at a little service station in Walkertown and parked the wrecker to take a short break. While we were resting, a truck driver I knew from Kernersville, who drove for a trucking company in Winston-Salem, had just finished a trip from up north and had hitched a ride from Winston-Salem to Walkertown. A fellow driver had dropped him off at this service station, and he was looking for a ride back to Kernersville. I told him that we would take him to Kernersville after we finished our work in Stanleyville. I gave him a choice to either ride with me in the Sterling or ride with Charlie in his empty pickup. He chose to ride with me in the wrecker. While we were still talking, the wrecker began sliding sideways slowly from where it was parked to the other side of the road where we were standing. Fortunately, it stopped before hitting us. The truck driver could hardly believe it. I thought the truck driver would change his mind, but he still wanted to ride in the wrecker with me. We then left for Stanleyville.

We soon arrived on the scene, and this turned out to be an easy job. We got the tractor and trailer back on the road and headed back to Kernersville. On Highway 66 in front of a restaurant, the wrecker slipped off the right side of the road into a ditch. The new non-directional tires on the front of the wrecker and the front-wheel drive helped pull us out, and we headed home.

We arrived at Stuart Motor Company around dawn the following day. Charlie suggested we put a tire chain on the right front tire. This stabilized the front of the wrecker as the tandem had a tendency to push the front around. We wished we had done this before leaving the previous day!

The truck driver had driven up north for many years in all kinds of weather, and Charlie and I had many experiences on ice, but we all agreed this had been the slickest night ever!

Psalm 147:17 "He casteth forth his ice like morsels: who can stand before his cold?"

Chapter 45. **Tell Me What To Do and I Will Do It**

It was early one Sunday morning in the late 1950s. The police department called to say they needed a wrecker for an emergency call. There were no rescue squads in those days, and a wrecker man had the responsibility to do the right thing in every situation. I had planned to play golf that Sunday and enjoy the day. I played after lunch but not until I had experienced a day of trauma and sadness.

When I arrived on the scene, an old Buick had hit a large sign post where two roads divide at Business 40 and Highway 421 at the Colfax exit. The car had bounced off the big sign and turned over onto its top. There were three passengers in the car, and all of them had been drinking. One person was pinned under the car. I checked him out and realized he was already dead. The second person was thrown out and seemed to be okay. The third occupant was impaled on the gear shift lever.

Mr. Roberts, a funeral home director, arrived on the scene with an ambulance. We looked at each other, and I asked him if I should pull the man off the lever or cut the lever off and leave it in his body for the doctor to remove. I said to Mr. Roberts, "Tell me what to do and I will do it!" He replied that he wasn't sure what to do either. (I thought he should know what to do since he was an experienced ambulance driver.)

Someone needed to do something quickly. I made a gut-wrenching decision, and I pulled the man off the gear shift and helped Mr. Roberts load him into the ambulance to go to the hospital. (I found out later the gear shift was not stuck straight into the man's chest like I thought it was. It had only appeared that way. The gear shift had gone in sideways into the fatty muscle of his chest. I was thankful that I had made the right decision.)

I could smell alcohol in the car. These three men made a bad choice: to drink and to drive drunk. They obviously couldn't make up their minds which road to take and had hit the sign post between the two roads. There are two roads and two destinies: you can accept Christ or reject Him.

Matthew 7:13-14 "Enter ye in at the strait gate: for wide is the gate, and broad is the way, that leadeth to destruction, and many there be which go in thereat: Because strait is the gate, and narrow is the way, which leadeth unto life, and few there be that find it."

Chapter 46. **The Trouble With Trains**

A train approaching a railroad crossing is almost a subtle thing. I used to think that anyone who got hit by a locomotive was quite foolish. How in the world could anyone miss seeing a big thing like a train? I will have to confess that I pulled this dumb trick, not once, but twice in 59 years. That makes me, according to my own estimation, twice as dumb! The first time I made this mistake was when

I had an urgent call one morning while I was on the way to Beck's Frame and Alignment Shop in Kernersville to tow a truck for them. I had just installed four new recapped rear tires on the rear axle of the Autocar. I had a bad habit of slowing down at a railroad crossing, first looking to the right to see if anything was coming, then looking to the left. If nothing was coming, I thought I was free to proceed on without stopping in order to save a little time. I was what the police call a "roll-on." I would talk to myself saying, "It's clear on the right; now I have time to stop if something is coming on the left!" How foolish! I do not remember how long I had been practicing this habit, but on this particular day, I had a BIG surprise waiting for me. As I approached the railroad crossing on Dobson Street in Kernersville, I looked to the right and then to the left. I did not hear a whistle, probably because the Autocar wrecker I was driving had a loud muffler on the side of the cab. All of a sudden, a train was right in front of me!

It scared me so much that I was off the seat pushing on the brake pedal with all my weight. I had pushed the brake pedal so hard, I thought it went through the floorboard. At the same time, I turned the steering wheel to the left as quick as I could to miss the train. My heart was racing as I heard the tires scream on the Autocar. The Autocar came to a halt within inches of the train. I was expecting the engineer to come back and chew me out. I believe that two things worked in my favor and prevented the collision: my new recapped rear tires and my quick thinking in turning the wheels to the left at the last minute. However, I know that the Lord Jesus Christ undoubtedly saved my life, and He sent an angel to stop me in time. Acts 27:23 says, "For there stood by me this night the angel of God, whose I am, and whom I serve."

The second time I had an encounter with a train, I made the same stupid mistake. Since I didn't learn my lesson the first time, it almost cost me my life again. This time I was driving my pickup truck instead of the wrecker. I had just left my friend Kenny Clark's house in Colfax and started to cross the railroad tracks at Highway 421. Because of the odd angle at the railroad crossing, I looked to the left first this time. Everything was clear, but when I looked to the right as I started to cross the tracks, a train was staring me in the face! The enormous train's headlights were bearing down on me and we were on a collision course. I could hardly believe I was doing the same foolish thing I had done years ago. History was repeating itself, and *I almost became history!* Slamming on the brakes of the pickup so forcefully caused the engine to cut off. I was so close to the train that I tried to crank up my pickup and back up as soon as possible, expecting part of the train to crash into the front of my truck, but it just missed me. How much closer to a train can you get? It seemed like I sat shaking in my seat forever. I looked around to see if anyone had witnessed this embarrassing situation. No one was around, but I realized the Lord had been watching over me again! I prayed and thanked Him for the marvelous grace He showed to one of His own! What a privilege to belong to Him and be called a Christian—all by grace! I finally learned my lesson regarding railroad crossings and since that time, I have always stopped, looked and listened.

Job 33:14 "For God speaketh once, yea twice, yet man perceiveth it not."

Chapter 47. **The Big Water Tank**

Dennis Medeiros, a brother in Christ, called me and wanted to know if I could bring my wrecker to Collinsville, Virginia and upright a water tank. The company that delivered the tank had left it on its side. Since the site was about 65 miles away in the state of Virginia, I quickly made up my mind that there was no way I was going to drive the old Sterling 40 mph that far. However, the site was a Bible camp for young people, and since this was a call from the Lord to help with His work, I felt that I needed to figure out a way to do the job. A crane would be too expensive.

I started asking Dennis a lot of questions about the job. When a wrecker man asks a lot of questions, he doesn't always get the best answers because every person has a different opinion. My wife couldn't understand why I asked so many questions on particular jobs. Getting as much information as possible could save a lot of time and mean the difference between success or failure, life or death. I asked Dennis if there were any trees close by. He said there were many oak trees and medium sized pines approximately 12 inches in diameter. They were located just where I needed an anchor. I had to set the water tank on a crushed rock platform that was built as a base for it. I was scheduled to arrive on a Saturday. I asked my friends, Leo Whicker and Charlie Barnard, to go with me in my four-wheel drive pickup truck loaded with snatch blocks, chains, one-half inch cable and clevises.

After having breakfast in Stoneville, we arrived and went to work. The tank had two brackets, one on each side—perfect for a pair of hooks with a ring in the middle. I climbed a tree and put a chain around it about 10 feet up making a "boom." I had to reinforce this "boom" with another tree behind it because the tree was small. This made an excellent anchor. However, there is really only one perfect anchor, the Lord Christ!

I doubled back twice from the "boom" to the tank and back. The end of the cable went to the back of my Ford truck. I put it in all-wheel drive and low range and slowly started down the hill. As I looked back, I saw two things: the tree anchor (the "boom") was bending, and the tank was coming up above the small trees. If my anchor held, it would do the job, but I wondered if it would fall properly on the crushed rock platform. Fortunately, the anchor held, and the tank set down in a perfect position. I thanked the Lord for the victory!

Hebrews 6:19 "Which hope we have as an anchor of the soul, both sure and steadfast, and which entereth into that within the veil..."

Chapter 48. **Would You Air Up My Tire?**

My pager went off around 7:00 one morning and woke me up out of a dead sleep. When I got a call during this time of the morning, it was hard to get up and get going full speed. The call involved a tractor and trailer which was blocking a road and was ready to turn over into a deep ditch. I thought it would be better to take the Autocar because it was faster.

When I arrived, the tractor was on the road, but the right rear of the loaded trailer had fallen into the ditch and was in danger of turning over. The front of the trailer was embedded in the outside tire of the tractor. When I saw the situation, I knew I had brought the wrong wrecker. I didn't have time to go back and get the Sterling, so I had to make the best of a bad situation because the road was blocked. I looked for a good anchor and saw a solid tree across the road. The road was already blocked on one side, so I decided to block the entire road. I took a five-eighths inch sling which was 30 feet long and tied it off to the tree. The Lord placed it exactly where I needed it.

There was a lot of pressure on me because the road was blocked in both lanes, and school buses were trying to get to the high school on time. Suddenly, an elderly woman walked up and asked, "Would you air up the tire on my car?" I could not believe she thought I had time to stop and air up her tire, but it made me laugh and it released some of the tension I was under. I told her I would be glad to help her, but it would be a while. This inspired me to finish the job. Sometime later, I saw a friend of mine who drove a garbage truck for the town of Kernersville, and I told him about this story. Every time I saw him after that, he would always ask me the same question, "Would you air up my tire?" and we would laugh. In the wrecker business, you have to have a sense of humor!

Philippians 4:11 "Not that I speak in respect of want: for I have learned, in whatsoever state I am, therewith to be content."

Chapter 49. **Mr. Patience**

Do you have any patience? What is patience? The Bible tells us that God is the God of patience (Romans 15:5). In the Hebrew epistle, the author tells us we have need of patience. In II Peter 1:5-6, the Bible tells us to add to your faith, patience.

We all need patience, especially a wrecker man. We may or may not learn patience from trials we experience. I might have had it one day and lost it the next day in a split second depending on the patrolman, the driver or the sidewalk supervisor.

One of my customers hauled earthmover tires in his pickup truck. This man had exceptional patience. He would tell his helper to take the end of a rope in his right hand and tie the first tire to the rack on the front of the bed of the pickup. Then the man would ask his helper if he understood what he had told him up to this point. If his helper said, "Yes," the man would go to the next procedure which was the second tire. At first, this seemed ridiculous because it would seem that anyone could tie two tires down to the bed of his pickup without a lot of instruction. But "Mr. Patience" was going to do it his way no matter how long it took his helper to learn how to tie a rope and to make sure he did it right. What motivated this man? Why did he seemingly waste so much time? Why did he have so much patience? After the second job I did for him, I found out the answer. He had experienced a severe heart attack, and he could not allow himself to get upset or rushed. I have experienced all kinds of situations. When I got upset, I tried to remember my customer. This is the reason I named him "Mr. Patience." Maybe we all should remember "Mr. Patience" because it might save our life. Why die before our time?

James 1:3-4 "Knowing this, that the trying of your faith worketh patience. But let patience have her perfect work, that ye may be perfect and entire, wanting nothing."

Chapter 50. **Black Ice**

All wrecker operators have probably experienced black ice. Driving on black ice can teach us some valuable lessons. It could be a fatal lesson. It doesn't matter who a person is or what type of vehicle he is in, how good a driver he thinks he is or how much experience he has—black ice has no mercy on anyone. I drove on a lot of it when I was in the Army in Alaska and when I was on many wrecker calls.

The Kernersville Fire Department received a call to go to Highway 421 on a freezing, cold morning. The young driver of the fire truck, I surmised, was probably excited and wanted to get to the destination as soon as possible. However, a thin sheet of black ice had formed on the highways—a subtle thing. This was the situation when the fire truck started to lose traction and proceeded to go down the steepest embankment in Kernersville. I would compare it to a front tire blowing out, and instantly, the vehicle is out of control. Since this was in the city limits, it was probably embarrassing for the fire department.

I got the call and headed to the scene. The dispatcher cautioned me that the highways were as slick as glass. I had to park and operate on a sheet of ice. I chose to anchor to a tree opposite the fire truck down the other side of the embankment. It was a long, drawn-out job because it was bitter cold and dangerous for me to go down the embankment to do my rigging. I was winching at an extreme right angle. If my anchor line had broken, I would have been in trouble. I had to let my anchor tree take most of the pull. Everything went well, and I winched the fire truck back up on the road.

The valuable lesson I learned in this episode was twofold: first, don't get in a bad situation to start with, and second, always keep up with the weather conditions.

II Timothy 3:14 "But continue thou in the things which thou hast learned and hast been assured of, knowing of whom thou hast learned them..."

Chapter 51. **How Do You Know?**

Years ago, I remember asking my dad this question, "How do you know?" His answer was, "How do I know anything?" This gave me something to ponder. I had always tried to make sure I rigged my cables correctly, so when I started a hard pull, there would be no damage, and most of all, no one would get injured. There are times when a wrecker man has to take a calculated risk. I had gambled a few times, only when I believed no one would get hurt; but if there was a possibility someone might get injured, I wouldn't take a chance.

Occasionally, something unforeseen would happen. Once I was winching a soft drink truck back on a bridge when a strap broke, and the cable flew back toward the operator of another wrecker beside me. It barely missed his head. He should have been at the controls on the other side of his wrecker out of the line of fire. I had all I could handle winching from my wrecker. I was responsible for putting the strap on, so I would have felt guilty if he had been injured.

I had put the strap around the front axle of the tractor, which was up in the air hanging over the creek below. The reason I used a strap in the first place was because a chain was too heavy to climb with and hook around the axle. This could have been a fatal mistake. I was doing a hard pull with my wrecker and never dreamed the nylon band would break. The pull on the strap was minimal, just enough to keep the tractor in line. I later found out the strap had somehow been cut. A wrecker man has to be knowledgeable, but how can he know everything?

I John 5:13 says, "These things have I written unto you that believe on the name of the Son of God; that ye may know that ye have eternal life." What things? To a wrecker man, knowing certain things from experience might save his life. To the sinner, he needs to know the gospel because it will save his soul for eternity. That I may know Him...this is the most important thing. The blind man in the Bible realized this when he said, "...One thing I know, that, whereas I was blind, now I see" (John 9:25).

Jeremiah 24:7 "And I will give them a heart to know me, that I am the Lord: and they shall be my people, and I will be their God: for they shall return unto me with their whole heart."

Chapter 52. **Nuts**

White Motor Company called and wanted me to tow two new long wheelbase trucks to Charlotte. I called Ronnie McKnight, my helper, to go with me. We arrived at the company and hooked up both trucks and headed to Charlotte. About six miles above Winston-Salem, I noticed that the truck Ronnie was towing was moving back and forth in a strange way. Since we did not have cell phones in those days, I started blinking my lights off and on to get Ronnie's attention, and he pulled over. We got out and soon found the problem. The nuts were missing on both front wheels with the exception of one or two.

The mystery of the missing nuts was solved when we returned to Kernersville. We were told by the company that the night before we had picked up the trucks, someone had stolen all the tires and wheels off the back. The company put new ones on the back so we could leave, but no one remembered to check the front wheels to see if all the nuts were still there! The thieves had started to take the front wheels off but were interrupted or scared off. I included this story to warn every wrecker man to always check his wheels to make sure all the nuts are tight before leaving on a call. A life might be saved, and that could include his own!

Proverbs 22:3 "A prudent man foreseeth the evil, and hideth himself: but the simple pass on, and are punished."

Chapter 53. **The Pipe Nipple**

My dad and I started to Mt. Airy to help Louie Taylor and his dad, some friends of ours, who ran Taylor's Garage. They wanted us to help them set up a 35 foot tank on its end at an oil company on Highway 601. One of us winched the tank upright while the other wrecker kept it in place to prevent it from falling the other way. At the end of the day, my job was to climb up and remove all the chains. As I took the hook loose from the chains, I forgot how many chains we had wrapped around the tank and how much they weighed (about 150 pounds)! The hook grabbed my glove, and I started to slide with the chains over the side of the tank. At the top of the tank, there was a pipe nipple that I could grip. By the grace of God I had enough strength to pull the chains up slightly where I could wiggle my hand out of the glove. The pipe nipple saved my life!

I like to think the Lord put it there just for me. He had more years for me to witness for Him. I was a teenager then, and I am 77 now! Hang onto the verse below; it is much better than an old pipe nipple!

Psalm 119:117 "Hold thou me up, and I shall be safe: and I will have respect unto thy statutes continually."

Chapter 54. **I Can Kill A Bear**

I had just gotten home from church when the phone rang. The man on the other end of the line asked me, "Mr. Stuart, are you still working?" I told him I was. He said he had a big trackhoe stuck up near Stokesdale. I told him I would come take a look at it. When I arrived, I saw that the trackhoe was buried deep in the mud. I told him I would return in approximately an hour with my equipment. The owner had hired a large, rough-looking, bearded guy who worked for the state to operate the trackhoe. The operator asked me if I could get the trackhoe out. I have always liked a challenge and this was a big one! Every once in a while, when I felt very confident about a job, I would tell the customer, "I can kill a bear if nobody bothers me!" When athletes feel confident, they say they are in the "zone."

I called my "shovel man," Jerry Wilkes, who once helped me recover an Eastern Airlines plane back on the runway. Jerry was a hard worker who could shovel for several hours. I called my son, Russ, to go with us. Jerry and Russ brought my pickup truck with large one inch and seven-eighths inch cable slings and some other equipment.

Everything went as planned, and we had the trackhoe out in four hours. It was dark, and I was making out the bill when the trackhoe operator walked up to my pickup and knocked on the window. I could not imagine what he wanted as he was not very polite when I had first arrived and had told him that I could kill a bear!

He said, "Mr. Stuart, do you remember when you arrived on the scene and told me you could kill a bear?" I replied, "Yes, sir," but had no clue what he was up to. Then he remarked, "You did it, and I sure do thank you. You made a believer out of me!" I did get a little respect, and I think the Lord did too because of the scripture verse on the back of my wrecker: Romans 5:8 ("But God commendeth his love toward us, in that, while we were yet sinners, Christ died for us.")

Philippians 4:13 "I can do all things through Christ which strengtheneth me."

Chapter 55. The Plan

This is one of my favorite stories. It involves the question the head DOT (Department of Transportation) supervisor asked when he arrived on the scene of a rollover involving a tractor and trailer on the new I-40 bypass near Kernersville. The rig was turned over the wrong way next to an embankment. This meant that the rig had to be turned back over toward the embankment. In order for the rig to come down flat, the embankment had to be cut back. My "Bobcat man," Kenny Clark, arrived on the scene with two helpers, Abraham and Jimmy. I told Kenny to cut the bank down while I put the Sterling at the rear of the trailer and another wrecker at the front of the trailer.

It was at this point that the DOT supervisor came up to Abraham and asked him in an official tone, "What is the plan?" Abraham replied in a low drawl, "I dunno." He then approached Jimmy and asked him the same question and got the same answer. Jimmy replied, "I dunno." We turned the rig back on its wheels, hooked up and towed it away. I told Kenny to stay behind and landscape the embankment to look like it did before we had cut it back. He did this in a precise and professional manner.

Kenny told me later that while I was busy rigging and supervising the operation, the DOT supervisor approached him and said, "I have worked accidents from Tennessee to South Carolina, and this has been the best operation I've ever seen!" This was a great compliment, especially since no one knew what the plan was! We all got a big laugh out of this! If I had known about his comment, I would have gladly told him that the Lord Christ was in charge; it was His plan, and I just went along with it!

Proverbs 16:3 "Commit thy works unto the Lord, and thy thoughts shall be established."

Chapter 56. **Threatened By A Gun**

A woman called me around 4:00 one morning and told me her car was stuck in a ditch. It seemed I got a majority of my calls early in the morning hours when I had to get out of my warm bed, get dressed and go out in the cold. The location was Highway 66 and Old Salem Road in Kernersville. I pulled up to the car and hooked a chain in the frame and winched it out onto the road. I made out the bill for $15. That was the going price in the 1960s. (That seems ridiculous now! The wrecker industry has come a long way.) The woman rolled her window down, and for the first time, I saw a man in the passenger seat of the car who I presumed was her husband. All of a sudden, the man pulled a gun out of the glove compartment and shouted at me, "The price is too high!" It startled me and rattled my nerves. As I considered what to do, I saw a little boy about six years old asleep in the back seat, covered up with a blanket. I then realized the man was drunk.

Even when I was a military policeman in the Army during the Korean War, I never experienced a situation quite like this. At that moment, I was not particularly happy since I had gotten out of bed in the middle of the night to help some woman stuck in a ditch and then be threatened with a gun by a foolish drunk. I thought about giving him a lecture, but that would probably have caused him to get more upset. After all, it is difficult to know what a drunk might do. I considered the little boy and everything changed. I did not want anyone to get hurt. I also remembered a verse from Proverbs 21:23 which says, "Whoso keepeth his mouth and his tongue keepeth his soul from troubles." I respectfully told the man, "Sir, I am glad I could help you folks," and I got in my wrecker and went back to my house and my warm bed. No pay, no vengeance. I felt good because I had honored the Lord.

Proverbs 20:3 "It is an honour for a man to cease from strife: but every fool will be meddling."

A Race Well Run

A RACE WELL RUN

My old Sterling wrecker and I have been running a race for many years. I have always said, "Whoever wears out first will have to stop." There is usually a winner in a race, but this race was a tie. We both had enough, so we stopped before we wore out.

A verse comes to mind about the children of Israel and how their shoes never wore out. "And I have led you forty years in the wilderness: your clothes are not waxen old upon you, and thy shoe is not waxen old upon thy foot" (Deuteronomy 29:5).

The wrecker ended the race in great shape. I may be a little worn, but after all, I am 10 years older than my Sterling.

Hebrews 12:1 "Wherefore seeing we also are compassed about with so great a cloud of witnesses, let us lay aside every weight, and the sin which doth so easily beset us, and let us run with patience the race that is set before us..."

Epilogue
EPILOGUE

BY REBECCA W. STUART

How To Survive Being A Wrecker Man's Wife

I've thought a lot about how to live with a wrecker man without becoming a wreck myself (mainly because I've had to). I'm a structured person and a perfectionist, one who plans and organizes. I like to be on time, eat on time, have a place for everything and everything in its place. Being married to a wrecker man for 52 years has somewhat changed that. I should have known that after dating this man for 10 years. He was never on time, or he might not show up at all because he would be somewhere else turning up a tractor and trailer. Plans were put on hold. For a special occasion, I might buy a new outfit and be ready to go but didn't get to.

My husband is a people person. I've kept truck drivers overnight who were total strangers, people from Guatemala who only spoke Spanish and who we could only communicate with through the Bible. We sat around the table singing a hymn, they, in Spanish, we, in English. We kept missionaries, doctors and preachers. Once we kept a minister's wife, a widow, for six weeks. Guests would come and go. Sometimes I felt like I had fed an army. There was always a new experience, mostly good, and the lessons we learned from them were invaluable.

A surgeon from Vancouver, Washington, who was a missionary in Nigeria, was one such visitor. I can see him now making himself at home, swinging in the yard and eating an apple like a small boy would enjoy. When he returned to Nigeria, he and a nurse from Greensboro were in a jeep that turned over into a rain-swollen creek, and they were both killed. They were on a mission to help others. Then, we also had the pleasure of meeting a minister who hitchhiked across the country preaching the gospel for 33 years and was never late for a meeting. Imagine that! As young Christians, my husband and I were stimulated by these people to love the scriptures and to live for our Savior, the Lord Jesus Christ.

I did not realize my life would be so diversified. I was slowly becoming more flexible. After having two children, a son and a daughter, being a structured perfectionist became harder and harder. I slowly learned to let go, but it was always work, work and more work. You see, when you are married to a wrecker man and need him the most, he is somewhere else. I tried to take as much responsibility off of Robert that I could. He was running a business and for 26 years, caring for his dad, who had a stroke five years after we were married. I took care of the children, the house and the yard. I've raked tons and tons of leaves and loaded them on a trailer, so my husband would have something to do when he got home! (I'm sure he was looking forward to that!) I also took care of the finances and book-keeping for the business. Sixteen years of banking experience had helped prepare me for this.

For many years, we went without a vacation. Occasionally, it was possible for him to take a day off to enjoy a game of golf. I learned to feed the children first, then eat by myself and keep his meals warm. I cooked three good meals every day because my husband loves delicious food, and he needed it for strength. It is good that I grew up on a nearby farm with hardworking parents who also made their seven children work. They taught me to be independent and responsible.

A wrecker man's hours are as bad or worse than a doctor's. It is twenty-four/seven, rain or shine, sleet or snow—you gotta go! You live from paycheck to paycheck which could often be weeks or months while waiting for customers to pay. My husband did many jobs for free. If someone could not afford to pay, or had really bad luck, he came home with an empty wallet. I may have had my hands in pie dough, and he would get a call. It was stop, fix a snack to go, get the thermos ready, make some quick phone calls, get the proper clothes ready and stay out of his way at the same time. It was a riot when he got two or three wrecker calls at the same time. Needless to say, I was never bored! I enjoyed my alone and quiet time, which I got occasionally.

Every January, when we had our little "board meeting" in the office, we sat at Robert's dad's double-sided antique desk that I refinished—Rob on his side and me on mine. We would look at each other and say, "Well, what are we going to do this year?" It was an old joke. We would continue to do the same thing one more year—every year.

Although my husband was one of the best riggers and recovery men who was well known and respected in the industry, he took time to be a wonderful husband, father and grandfather. He also visited and ministered to others and shared his testimony.

We all survived his overprotective nature. I suppose most wrecker men are overprotective, since everything they do is dangerous. Our daughter, Anna, who is now 38 years old, reminds her dad that she never saw any lions in the street. Our son, Russ, who is 40 years old, has to continually show him how to operate all the TVs, DVDs, VCRs and all the gadgets on modern day cars. Any man who can operate a 1943 Sterling and set eight airplanes back on the runway should be able to handle these small tasks!

At our age, I think it is time to slow down. We enjoy our three grandchildren: Rally, Collin and Carlee, who live close by. They ride their bicycles through the field, down by the garden. Our daughter-in-law, Audrey Dee, started strolling the children down this path when they were babies. Now she makes sure they get to the parades and truck shows. Our grandchildren bring us much joy, and we are spending more time with them. We live on 15 acres of green pastures and creeks, a great place for them to play.

After much persuasion from his family, Robert retired on Thanksgiving Day 2007. We all took turns ringing the dinner bell. Robert doesn't scream when the phone rings anymore, and our lives are much calmer.

It's amazing; I still love this man after 52 years of marriage. In the Bible, it says love never fails, and I have found that to be true. I am proud of my husband for all he accomplished during his career, and I am thankful to the Lord for always keeping him safe. I am also grateful to the Lord for maintaining my sanity while I was running the household. My husband was involved in wrecks on a daily basis, but at least he did not have to come home to one. As far as I know, I am still intact.

-Rebecca W. Stuart

Ephesians 5:33 "Nevertheless let every one of you in particular so love his wife even as himself; and the wife see that she reverence her husband."

Glossary

GLOSSARY

air wand- A piece of pipe that is placed deep in the mud in which compressed air is forced through to relieve suction from around the object you are winching out.

clevis- A U-shaped device with a bolt or pin passing through holes at the two ends for joining two cables together.

cribbing- A framework of wood blocks or plywood to support heavy equipment.

dead legs- Strong steel tubings used on the back of a wrecker or trailer to stabilize it.

double back- To take a cable to a certain location where you put it through the pulley of a snatch block and take the cable back to the original point or another location for a mechanical advantage.

drag line- An excavating machine with a boom on a rotating platform and cables for controlling a bucket.

fifth wheel- A device that is used to hook a road tractor to a trailer.

jiff lock- A single axle dolly with dual wheels which has a tongue on the front and a fifth wheel on top and is used to attach twin trailers together.

pintle hook- A sturdy device that opens up to receive a trailer hitch.

pipe nipple- A short piece of pipe with threads on each end.

pup trailer- Two short trailers usually hooked together.

rigging- A procedure using cables and snatch blocks to move equipment from one location to another.

scotch- A block placed under a wheel to prevent moving or slipping.

sheave- A pulley with a groove around it which will receive a wire rope cable.

shim- To shorten the distance from a winch to the piece of equipment you are trying to recover. This is done by using one or two big cables hooked together from that piece of equipment to a certain point.

snatch block- A steel block with a hook on the end, with a pulley inside, that is used for winching.

winch- A machine with a spool of cable powered mechanically for lifting or pulling.

Romans 5:8

"But God commendeth his love toward us, in that,
while we were yet sinners, Christ died for us."